The Basics of Traditional Chinese Culture

Compiled by: Zhi E'xiang

Foreign Languages Press Beijing

First Edition 2005

ISBN 7-119-03904-0

© Foreign Languages Press, Beijing, 2005
Published by Foreign Languages Press
24 Baiwanzhuang Road, Beijing 100037, China
Distributed by China International Book Trading Corporation
35 Chegongzhuang Xilu, Beijing 100044, China
P. O. Box 399, Beijing, China

Printed in the People's Republic of China

Splendid Chinese Culture: An Introduction

In his famous work *Science and Civilization in China,* Dr. Joseph Needham, an outstanding British expert of scientific history in modern times, commented that if one did not think it too troublesome to read through his voluminous book, he was sure one would find surprisingly that Europe had absorbed varied and colorful technologies from China. Francis Bacon, father of modern Western science, also admitted that China's three inventions—printing, gunpowder and compass—had changed the face of the whole world.

China had really been one of the great centers of human civilization, science and technology for many centuries, having written a brilliant chapter in the world's cultural history, which we may see from the following examples:

China was well known for its agricultural civilization. Rice and corn—present-day world's major food grains—were first cultivated by Chinese ancestors in the Yangtze and Yellow River valleys 7,000-8,000 years ago.

China was the "origin of silk." As far back as 5,000 years ago, Chinese ancestors had mastered the skill of raising silkworms, and that of reeling and weaving silk. Over 200 silk and linen fabrics were unearthed in the No.1 Tomb of the Han Dynasty at Mawangdui, in Changsha City, Hunan Province, in 1972, including an intact plain gauze unlined garment, which was soft, bright, and as thin as a cicada's wings, fully showing China's superb weaving art of 2,100 years ago. Way back in the Han (206 B.C.-220 A.D.) and Tang (618-907 A.D.) dynasties Chinese silk fabrics had continuously flowed to West Asian and European countries, winning great favor with the people there.

Known as the "birthplace of tea," China was the first country to plant tea and use it as a beverage. As far back as 2,700 years ago, Shen Nong discovered the detoxicating function of tea, and used it to cure diseases. People started to drink tea in the Han Dynasty. Chinese tea found its way to Japan, Korea and some other countries in the fifth century, and sold to the European and American nations in the 17th century. Henceforth tea drinking had become popular all over the world. The savory Chinese tea, which is beneficial both to improving one's intelligence and preserving one's health, has become one of the three most important drinks in the world, on a par with coffee and cocoa.

Known as the "home of chinaware," China was the first country to invent porcelain. The "primitive celadon" was baked in the Zhou Dynasty over 3,000 years ago. During the Tang Dynasty, porcelain production entered a varied and colorful stage. The celadon produced in the Yue Kiln during the period was as green as jade, and was an important item on China's export list. China had become one of the most civilized and rich countries in the world during the Tang Dynasty, a period of great prosperity, when envoys, students, businessmen and monks from Asian and African countries gushed into China as tidewater. Situated in the central part of Asia, China was in frequent contacts with other nations, becoming a bridge linking Asia, Africa and Europe. All this had provided convenience for the export of porcelains. Chinese porcelains were spread westward along the "Silk Road" developed in the Han Dynasty, i.e., from Xinjiang to Persia, Syria, as far as to the Mediterranean countries. It reached Korea and Japan either directly from the northeast, or along the sea route from Mingzhou (modern Ningbo), Yangzhou and Quanzhou. In the Tang Dynasty, a maritime trade commissioner was appointed in Guangzhou to supervise navigation and shipbuilding, as well as foreign trade. Guangzhou became an important port, where merchants from home and abroad thronged. Starting from there, one might reach Southeast Asian countries, or get to the Persian Gulf, the Mediterranean coast, Egypt and Syria by rounding the Malay Peninsula. As porcelain was an important export product, scholars called the navigation route the "Porcelain Road."

The Chinese ancestors had created one age of civilization after another, as well as varied, colorful and complete material and intellectual cultures, covering fields ranging from metallurgy, papermaking, printing, gunpowder, compass, astronomy and mathematics to costume, tea ceremony and cuisine, and from philosophy, institutions and systems to ethics, morals and social customs. The thousands-of-years-old history of Chinese culture is replete with splendid achievements, clearly showing China's contributions to world civilization and its friendly contacts with other peoples. From it we seem to be able to hear the clear and melodious sound of camel bells on the "Silk Road" and catch glimpses of the sails of ships gliding on the vast expanses of green water. Today, China is opening its door to sincerely welcome friends from afar. When you appreciate the magnificent views atop the Great Wall, seek your old dreams in front of the Hall of Supreme Harmony in the former Imperial Palace in Beijing, visit the massive terracotta army of Emperor Qin Shi Huang in Xi'an, or taste the delicious Beijing roast ducks, you will feel that China's long-standing, unified and continuous traditional culture is still shining brilliantly.

It is universally known that human labor is a creative activity carried out in accordance with the rules of beauty. The tens of thousands of artifacts with historical, scientific and artistic values are embodiments of beauty. This book includes 22 special topics, including the achievements of the Chinese people in material and cultural fields. The authors, who are all experts of traditional Chinese culture, have tried their best to explain the broad and profound contents of Chinese culture in vivid and popular language. To really understand a nation, one must get to know its culture and tradition. It is our hope, therefore, that this book will lead the readers to the palace of traditional Chinese culture to understand a great nation through appreciating the mysterious and interesting cultural views, both old and new.

Contents

The Yellow Emperor and the Dragon Culture   1

Confucius and Confucianism   6

Taoism and Traditional Chinese Culture   11

The Influence of Buddhism on Traditional Chinese Culture   16

The Lord Guan Culture and Lord Guan Temple   21

A General View of Traditional Chinese Medicine   26

The Magic of Acupuncture and Moxibustion   33

Qigong Breathing Exercise   36

Probing the Mysteries of Wushu Martial Arts   40

Fascinating Chinese Characters   47

Tea and Teahouses   51

Alcoholic Drinks   59

Silk   63

Chinese Dress and Accessories in Various Periods   66

The Fan   76

Bamboo   83

Chopsticks   93

Traditional Chinese Musical Instruments   98

The "Four Treasures of the Study"   106

Chinese Ceramics   115

The Yellow Emperor and the Dragon Culture

The Yellow Emperor.

During the primitive clan commune period 5,000 years ago, two tribal chiefs—the Yellow Emperor and Yandi Emperor—lived in the Yellow River Valley. They were regarded as the earliest ancestors of the Chinese nation.

The original surname of the Yellow Emperor was Gongsun, and because he lived in the Jishui River area, he later changed it to Ji. He prospered on the Loess Plateau of Shaanxi Province, hence his name. Five thousand years ago the Yellow Emperor led his tribe to rise to the north of the Weishui River in Shaanxi Province, and then gradually to move eastward to reach the Yellow River bank in the southern part of Shanxi Province, and Zhuolu in Hebei Province.

The Yandi Emperor also prospered in areas to the east of Qishan

An early Western Zhou Dynasty bronze carving of a dragon.

Mountain in Shaanxi Province. Because he lived in the Jiangshui River area, he used Jiang as his surname. Compared with that of the Yellow Emperor, the Yandi Emperor's development route slanted south, extending eastward along the Weishui and Yellow rivers, reaching Henan and Shandong provinces, and then going southward to the Jianghan Plain and Hunan Province.

A bronze dragon carving from the Warring States Period.

Since both of them had created the ancient civilization of the Yangtze and Yellow river valleys, laying the foundation for the 5,000-year mansion of Chinese civilization, the Yandi and Yellow emperors were honored as the earliest Chinese ancestors by the Chinese people both at home and abroad.

During the process of the continuous multiplication and development of the clans and tribes, the Yandi tribe collided with the Jiuli tribe in the southeast. Yandi asked the Yellow Emperor for help when he was defeated. The Yellow and Yandi emperors then jointed

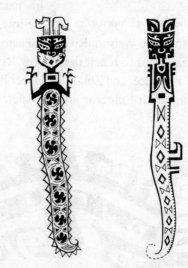

Bone carvings of a human head on a snake's body from the Yin Dynasty (late Shang Dynasty).

hands and defeated Chi You at Zhuolu. But then a battle broke out between the two former allies at Banquan, ending in the failure of Yandi. Finally, the Yellow Emperor was honored by the tribal chiefs as the leader of the tribal alliance formed at the meeting initiated by the Yellow Emperor, thus settling China's basic domain. The integration of the clans was accelerated in the post-war period, culminating in the formation of the Huaxia tribe, the main body of the Chinese nation.

Out of some cultural psychology and ideology, the Chinese ancestors created dragon, a cultural product which was actually non-existent. A great number of explanations and descriptions of the dragon can be found in ancient Chinese books. One says, "The entire body of the dragon was integral with different parts. Riding floating clouds, it nourished Yin and Yang." Another says, "The dragon, born in water and covered with five colors, could change into a tiny silkworm when it wanted to become small; change into a formidable giant when it wanted to become big; rise above the clouds when it wanted to go up; and sink to the bottom of a spring when it wanted to go down." Still another says, "Its horns looked like those of a deer; head, camel; eyes, ghost; neck, snake; scales, carp; talons, hawk; palms, tiger; and ears, ox." These descriptions show that, in ancient Chinese people's minds, the dragon was a mixture of various animals with no regular shape but with the abilities of raising winds and rains, soaring to the sky and diving to the bottom of a sea, and bestowing favors on all

An Eastern Han Dynasty stone carving found in Yinan in Shandong Province.

creatures on earth.

Why was the dragon so magical?

As far back as 5,000 years ago, each clan or tribe regarded a deity as its guardian god as well as its symbol, i.e., totemism. When a clan or tribe annexed another one, it would add its most distinctive symbol into its own to represent its victory. Therefore, the mixed shape of the dragon was actually an agglomerate of the totems characteristic of different clans in the formative stage of the Huaxia tribe, or the Chinese nation.

The dragon originated from the powerful Yellow Emperor tribe in the Central Plains, and finally took shape in the process of the merger of the various clans. With a strange shape, it had great magic power. It was regarded as one of the Four Auspicious Animals that could bring courage, strength and happiness to people. The other three auspicious animals were the unicorn (a legendary animal with the shape of a deer, with horns on the head, scales on the whole body and a tail); the phoenix (a legendary fowl with beautiful feathers, supposed to be the king of birds, the male ones being called *feng* and the female ones *huang*); and the miraculous turtle.

With its becoming the totem of the Yellow Emperor tribe and the

Different forms of the Chinese character *long* ("dragon") from different periods.

4

Yellow Emperor himself symbolizing unification and agglomeration, the dragon also became a symbol of unification and agglomeration.

Due to people's ardent love and worship of the Yellow Emperor, the dragon had become high in their favor, and the strong awareness of the dragon culture had penetrated deep into the various fields of Chinese culture for thousands of years. Buildings were named after the mythical beast, such as the Dragon Palace, Dragon Gate and Dragon Court, and decorated with dragon patterns, and artworks featured its dignified and grandiose images, imbuing them with great artistic charm and strong aesthetic appeal. There was also the Dragon Dance, Dragon Feast, Dragon Tea, and so on and so forth.

The ancestral emperor Xuanyuan (Yellow Emperor).

Even today, the dragon embodies people's ideals, wishes, wisdom and strength. It is also a symbol of the Chinese nation. For this reason, people of other nations refer to China as the "huge dragon in the East," and the "descendants of the Yandi and Yellow emperors" all over the world also proudly claim themselves to be the "decendants of the dragon."

Confucius and Confucianism

Confucius.

Confucius (551-479 B.C.) was a philosopher, political thinker and educator of ancient China, whose influence is still felt across the world.

Confucius lived in an era when China was rent by dozens of feudal states. Confucius was born in Zou of the State of Lu (modern Qufu, Shandong Province). He descended from a noble line in the State of Song, which had declined long before he was born. Confucius lost his father when he was three years old, which made his family fare from bad to worse. He was always fond of learning. In his younger days, he tended warehouses and cattle and sheep for other people, at the same time earning his living by managing wedding and funeral affairs for rich families. Therefore, he could get access to both the ordinary people to understand their sufferings and upper-class people to be familiar with their etiquette. He had also gradually mastered rich knowledge of ancient Chinese culture, becoming an erudite standing apart from his peers. He served as minister of justice in the State of Lu for a short term, during which he had many outstanding achievements to his credit.

An admirer of Duke Zhou, a great statesman of the Western Zhou Dynasty (11th century-771 B.C.), Confucius also wanted to introduce the political institutions developed by Duke Zhou to the State of Lu. However, due to the great social upheaval and the intensified contradictions between the upper and lower classes at that time, he could not realize his ideals, and he was very much upset. So he started to travel from state to state.

He ran into snags everywhere, failing to obtain an important post in any of those states. He had no alternative but to return to his native state when he reached the advanced age of 68. Since then, he had devoted himself to education. He widely recruited and cultivated students, breaking the "monopolization of learning by the government," and adding a splendid chapter in China's educational history. At the same time, he engaged in editing many classics, including *The Book of Songs, The Book of History, The Book of Rites,* and *The Book of Music,* making an everlasting contribution to spreading, sorting out and preserving the ancient cultural heritages. He died at the age of 73.

His students or even their students had recorded Confucius' lifetime words and deeds in *The Analects of Confucius*, which systematically reflected his thoughts and opinions. Many of his words have become famous adages often quoted by Chinese today.

Scholars have always agreed that "benevolence" (*ren*) is the core of Confucius' ideological system. The implications of the code of conduct, or the "rites" (*li*), he advocated at that time naturally covered some administrative systems, which had to be guaranteed by the concept of "benevolence." Asked about "benevolence," he replied, "It is to love all men." Asked about the way of realizing "benevolence," he proposed two principles, that is, that "You should not do to others what you would not have them do to you," and "Wishing to be established himself, one should also seek to establish others, while wishing to be enlarged himself, one should also seek to enlarge others." Worthy of special attention is that Confucius explicitly affirmed differences in social relations—difference between the close and the distant and between the high and the low. Therefore, there were differences in the love of the "benevolent." Of course, we cannot interpret Confucius' views out of the context of his era. We cannot claim that he was advocating the views of the modern Western world, such as the so-called "universal love" and "everyone being born with the inalienable rights of man." Nevertheless, one thing is certain, that he had sort of changed the ruling-class idea of treating the slaves as if they were beasts of burden, and openly opposed the "cruelty" of "putting the people to death without having instructed them." In this connection, his views contained elements of affinity to the people, progressiveness and rationality.

He also comprehensively summarized the ruling experience of the patriarchal hierarchical society, that the rulers should not forget to educate people in benevolence while practicing brutal tyranny so as to rid the ruled of the idea of "rebelling against the authority." The best course was to alternate severity with leniency, or the "rule by virtue." He openly opposed rulers riding roughshod over the people solely by power, believing it was unpopular to "rule by force," which the "benevolent" should definitely not practice.

Unlike Sakyamuni, Jesus Christ and Muhammad, Confucius was by no means a religious leader of ancient China. Although he "venerated the will of Heaven," he did not believe in the next life, nor did he believe in the existence of ghosts and spirits. He said: "While you do not know life, how can you know about life?" and "While you are not able to serve men, how can you serve their spirits?" The great modern Chinese writer Lu Xun gave a very high opinion on this when he said: "Confucius was a really great man. Although the belief in ghosts was very popular in his time, he would not swim with the tide." The liberal ideas had undoubtedly exerted profound influences in China, so that, after Confucius' thought had become official philosophy, later feudal rulers found it hard to control the people with religious ideas and to check the spread of ancient atheism. Some people attempted to turn "Confucian studies" into a "Confucian faith" on a par with Buddhism and Taoism, and even the Christian faith from the West. However, the attempt failed to become reality. As a result, religious beliefs in China had never overridden "politics" (royal authority), which was a unique characteristic of traditional Chinese culture.

As Confucius' most outstanding contribution to Chinese culture lay in education, he was called the "teacher of all ages" by the later generations, and became a "sage" in feudal society. He was the first to advocate the idea of "making no distinction of social status in teaching," breaking the past privilege of the nobles monopolizing culture and education, and expanding the social basis of education, which had played a very important role in promoting the inheritance, spread and development of ancient academic thinking. The Confucian canons produced by Confucius and his disciples, such as the "Five Classics" (*The Book of Songs*, *The Book of*

History, *The Book of Changes*, *The Book of Rites* and *The Spring and Autumn Annals*) and the "Four Books" (*The Analects of Confucius*, *The Great Learning*, *The Doctrine of the Mean* and *Mencius*), had become national-level required readings for intellectuals.

As education always serves a given political purpose, Confucius was no exception. His ideal that "Officialdom is the natural outlet for good scholars" was completely reasonable in the ancient time, when studies in special fields were not well developed. Compared with the practice of ruling the people by some nobles who had neither learning nor skill, and only idled away their time in pleasure-making, it was really a progressive new idea. However, Confucius opposed students engaging in agricultural production, for he believed that the main purpose of education was to reinforce and improve the social ruling order and ease the contradictions between the ruler and the ruled. Therefore, the disciples must learn to "administer a country."

However, being "insatiable in learning" and "tireless in teaching," and having engaged in education wholeheartedly over dozens of years, Confucius had summarized his correct and valuable experience to enlighten numerous scholars of great attainments, especially educators, of the later generations on the attitude toward study and ways of thinking. Adhering to a conscientious spirit of seeking knowledge, he held that "one should know what one really understands and admit what one does not know—this is knowledge," which was very similar to the opinion of the famous Greek philosopher Socrates. He also stressed that "If the name is not right, then speech will not be in order; and if speech is not in order, then nothing will be accomplished," a viewpoint that well reflected the special characteristics of his philosophy and established a lofty example of studiousness for the later generations by associating one's "name" with one's "speech," and one's "speech" with one's "action."

Confucius believed that only by "carrying forward the cause pioneered by the predecessors" could the people "forge ahead into the future," i.e., they should open up the new future without breaking the old tradition, which was another important characteristic of his thinking. Instead of blindly advocating the restoration of ancient ways, he believed that they should carry out concrete reforms by "increasing" or "decreasing" the old rules and regulations, but not by "destroying the old and establishing the new." In treating cultural heritages, he asked people to "review what has been learned" in order to "learn something new." Therefore, he paid great attention to drawing lessons from historical experience, as he put it in the words such as "I am not one who was born in the possession of knowledge; I am one who is fond of antiquity, and earnest in seeking it there." These sayings had somewhat helped later generations to attach importance to historical studies.

All schools of thought contended for attention in China after Confucius died. To meet the political needs arising from the realization of national unification, Liu Che, Emperor Wudi of the Western Han Dynasty (206 B.C.-25 A.D.), "banned all schools of thought and only venerated Confucianism." The "old liners" and "reformers" among the feudal scholars of the successive dynasties creatively elaborated the Confucian thought by "absorbing what they needed" from the materials of the Confucian School according to the social characteristics and ideologies of the various periods. This had resulted in the extraordinary complexity of the history of the Chinese study of Confucian classics, a complexity caused by the mingling of positive contributions, negative influence and even arbitrary distortions, so that, after continuous revisions over the centuries, it was difficult to judge which school represented the true features of the Confucian doctrine. At the present, some countries either praise or criticize "Neo-Confucianism." Due to association with the present practical problems of different natures, and the divergences of understandings, the situation has become even more complicated, so people will have to study it carefully from different angles. However, modern experts and scholars agree unanimously that in spite of its dross and negative elements, Confucianism, as a cultural heritage, will play a positive role in economic development and modernization in modern society so long as people act in the spirit of "discarding the false and retaining the true, destroying the old and establishing the new."

(by Shi Jun)

Taoism and Traditional Chinese Culture

Zhang Daoling, or Celestial Master Zhang.

Taoism is an indigenous Chinese religion. It formally appeared at the end of the Eastern Han Dynasty (25-220), taking Lao Zi as its founder and venerated deity, and *Dao De Jing*, or *Tao Te Ching* (*Classic of the Way and Virtue*) as its leading canon. Later, it listed the gradually developed personages of the Taoist philosophical school as its *Zhen Ren* (True Man, who has attained enlightenment or immortality through practicing Taoism), and included the Taoist works in the *Dao De Jing*. As a result, the scope of Taoism was expanded, covering both the immortality alchemy and the teachings of charm, and the Taoist philosophical school was lumped together with the Taoist religious faith. Today, besides the general term "Taoist school," there are also such appellations as the "immortals' school" and the "Lao Zi-Zhuang Zi studies." Taoist followers also call Taoism the "immortals' doctrine," "alchemists' doctrine" or the "Taoist school." When summarizing the major constituents of the history of Chinese thought, historians often mention "Confucianism, Buddhism, and Taoism" at the same time. Taoism in this connection refers to both the Taoist school and Taoist faith.

People often say that "Taoism attaches great importance to life, while

Buddhism to death." "Attaching great importance to life" refers to seeking the eternity of the human body and flying up to Heaven to become immortals, as manifested in the myth of "The Goddess Chang'e Flying to the Moon." The beautiful and touching story has circulated among the people through all ages, and become well-known to every household, reflecting the features and charms of "attaching great importance to life" of ancient Chinese culture.

Taoism developed the mythologies into the theory of becoming an immortal with the help of a corpse—leaving a dead body to give people the false impression that the person was dead, while the real flesh had secretly become an immortal. Many stories of ghosts and spirits told about people digging a dead person's tomb or opening the coffin after the person had died and been buried many days, only to find no corpse therein at all, but only a pair of shoes, a sword or a bamboo stick. Then they realized that the person had become an immortal with the help of the corpse. Such myth can also be found in Taoist classics. It can thus be seen that the core of the myth was still "attaching great importance to life."

According to a historical record, Zhang Guo, a famous Taoist, suddenly died when Emperor Xuanzong (r. 712-742) of the Tang Dynasty summoned him for an audience. His disciples buried his body, and the emperor had to give up. The people found that the corpse had gone when they opened the coffin later, then they realized that Zhang Guo had become an immortal with the help of his corpse to avoid being appointed to an official position by the emperor. Therefore, such mythologies sometimes implied rich social contents and profound morals.

Taoism claimed that the destination of immortals would definitely not be as lonely as in the Moon Palace. Besides enjoying themselves in the mortal world, they might also live happily in a "fairyland" or "paradise." The belief in immortality is not only a primitive belief of Taoism but it is also a consistent doctrine with distinctive Chinese characteristics.

According to Taoist teachings, Taoist followers should save not only themselves, but also others, including the deceased.

The philosophical basis of Taoist theology is for the most part formed by assimilating ancient Chinese philosophical thoughts of every description. It has absorbed the Tao (the Way) of the Taoist school as the supreme philosophical category, and its outlooks on nature and the world, the concept of changes and the Taiji (Supreme Ultimate) theory, as expressed in *The Book of Changes*, the divinatory symbols, the theory of cycles, the Yin-Yang theory and the theory of the Five Elements (metal, wood, water, fire and earth), as well as the *chen wei xue* (esoteric study of auguries and Confucianist texts for prophecies) of the Han Dynasty, and the Confucian ethical and moral standards.

A lot of contents of the Taoist theology were developed from ancient thoughts, including the witchcraft, nature worship and the religious concepts of the remote ages, such as the worship of the deities originated from the sun, moon, stars, rivers, lakes and seas, animals, etc.

The diversified Taoist beliefs lead to its colorful and extraordinarily enormous pantheon. Although originated from China, Taoist divinities vary greatly with historical and regional differences. The Pure Trinity—the Original Divinity (Yuanshi Tianzun), Treasure Divinity (Lingbao Tianzun) and Moral Divinity (Daode Tianzun)—have been generally worshipped as the supreme Taoist gods since the Yuan and Ming dynasties. Other categories include the gods of nature, immortals, and the ancestral gods—the founders or important inheritors of various sects.

As the alchemy for treating diseases and preserving health was closely related to traditional Chinese medicine, many Taoists were also famous experts in the field, such as Ge Hong of the Eastern Jin Dynasty (317-420); Tao Hongjing, the Liang Dynasty (502-557); and Sun Simiao, the Tang Dynasty (618-907). Persisting in the concept of preventive medicine, Ge Hong had made outstanding contributions to semeiology and therapeutics. Tao Hongjing had made remarkable achievements in the studies of herbal medicine and the science of health preserving, and also in the ancient theories of traditional Chinese medicine. Sun Simiao was honored as the King of Medicine by later generations for the achievements he had made in traditional Chinese medical theories and practice, and the sorting out of medical prescriptions.

The pills for external use in Taoism refer to those made of refined minerals such as cinnabar, lead and mercury, or added with Chinese medicinal herbs to become what are called elixirs of life. The alchemy of gold and silver, a variety of making the pills for external use, refer to the refinement of the cheap metalliferous minerals such as mercury, lead and iron to transform them into gold and silver—two precious metals. It was called golden pills at first, and later changed its name to pills for external use to distinguish from those for internal use. Although it is a fantastic illusion that one would live a long life and become an immortal by taking the pills for external use, some of them were really effective in curing diseases. During the refinement, gold and silver would sometimes be separated from the minerals, or the alloys resembling gold or silver could be obtained, playing an important role in promoting the development of metallurgical technologies, especially in the development of the ancient chemistry and the invention of gunpowder.

The pills for internal use refer to the "elixirs of life" refined in one's body by adjusting his thoughts and breath, taking his body as a cooking vessel or stove, and the vital essence in his body as the medicine. The practice is similar to the modern Qigong breathing exercise. According to Taoism, modern Qigong is only the basic stage of refining the pills for internal use, which includes many schools. Of course, one cannot become an immortal by taking the pills. However, as the practice emphasizes the studies of the human body, it is somewhat effective in curing one's diseases and improving one's health.

Most of the Taoist places of worship were called *guan* (temples), others palaces, convents, nunneries, monasteries, towers, caves, halls, or temples. Some people called large ones palaces, and small ones, temples; while others called the ones whose names were granted by emperors palaces, and the others, temples. Each view had its own basis, but one should not think in absolute terms. With historical changes, the fact that the names matched reality would also be changed. Most of the palaces and temples were constructed ancient Chinese style with symmetrical layouts, the inscribed boards and couplets setting off each other, and the numerous murals and carved tablets were lent a classic flavor. Some of them were imbued with Taoist doctrines, while others had unique architectural and aesthetic features. They are all centers of religious activities, and some have become the centers of temple fairs. For example, the White Cloud Temple in Beijing has hosted Spring Festival temple fairs in recent years, attracting tens of thousands of people.

In the Yuan Dynasty, a situation appeared, in which two major Taoist sects, the Quanzhen (All True) and the Zhengyi (Orthodox Unity), shared equal glory, and this has continued to the present day. The Quanzhen sect, founded by Wang Ji of the Jin Dynasty, emphasized cultivation of the spirit, or *nei xiu* (internal cultivation), and cultivation of assistance to the people, or *wai xiu* (external cultivation). Taoists of the Quanzhen sect neither married nor ate meat. The Zhengyi sect, founded by Celestial Master Zhang (Zhang Daoling, 34-156 A.D.) of Dragon and Tiger Mountain, valued charms and talismans. Taoists of the Zhengyi sect might marry and eat meat. Some of them lived in temples, while others lived at home, and were called scattered Taoists. The Taoist faith in both Taiwan and Hong Kong originated from the Chinese mainland, and belongs to the Quanzhen sect. Taoists of both Quanzhen and Zhengyi sects wear the same attire and observe the same lifestyle as in the ancient days.

(by Zhu Yueli)

The Influence of Buddhism on Traditional Chinese Culture

Founded by Sakyamuni during the sixth to fifth century B.C., Buddhism prospered during the reign period of Indian King Asoka, who used the equalitarian idea of "all living creatures are born with Buddha-nature" to unify southern India. However, after the seventh century, both Hinduism and Islam opposed Buddhism, destroying Buddhist temples and images of Buddhas and killing Buddhist believers. Buddhist followers fled to Sri Lanka in the south or to Tibet of China in the east. Neither Buddhist temples nor monks can be found in India today, and few Buddhist classics can be seen there. However, Buddhist scriptures and doctrines were widely propagated in China, so much so that Chinese-language scriptures were used in Korea and Japan.

Buddhism spread to the interior of China during the early Eastern Han Dynasty (25-220), followed by Buddhist scriptures and images and the translation of Buddhist scriptures. Besides the Sanskrit versions, some of the scriptures were translated from the languages of states in the Western Regions (roughly modern Xinjiang and Central Asia). The Venerable Xuan Zang, an eminent monk of the Tang Dynasty (618-907), went to India to seek Sanskrit scriptures. Upon return to China, he organized translation of the scriptures he had brought back. With the spread of Buddhism in China, changes began to take place in the form of Chinese writing. The ancient Chinese long narrative poem *Southeast Fly the Peacocks* was created under the influence of the long poem *Buddhacarita Kavyasutra*. The "Bianwen" (a form of narrative literature flourishing in the Tang Dynasty, with alternate prose and rhymed parts for recitation and singing), which was adopted to spread Buddhist doctrines, opened a new road for the development of the librettos or scripts of ballad-singers in vernacular.

Buddhist rallies became the recreational centers of trade caravans and market fairs.

Great changes had also taken place in the form of writing among upper-class people. A spate of works had flowed from the writing brush of eminent Buddhist monks, such as the full-length biographies *Life of Master Tripitaka of the Temple of Great Maternal Grace* and *Life of Fa Xian*, and the full-length travelogue *Buddhist Records of the Western World in the Tang Dynasty*. A lot of unprecedentedly magnificent scripts on Buddhist steles had also been produced since the Northern Wei Dynasty (386-534), including the *Preface to the Holy Religion of Tripitaka of the Great Tang*.

Buddhism had also exerted a great influence on Chinese art. At first, no image of Buddha was built. The worshippers only set up a seat and carved footmarks in front of it to symbolize a Buddha being seated there. People in the ancient State of Gandhata in north India used the Greek skill of creating statues to make the images of Buddhas. The figures with great originalities were first spread to the western border area of China. Some of them have been preserved till the present, such as the murals of the Kirzil Grottoes in Baicheng, the Thousand-Buddha Caves in Kuqu, and the Thousand-Buddha Caves in Senmsam—all in Xinjiang; the Mogao Grottoes in Dunhuang, Gansu Province; the Yungang Grottoes in Datong, Shanxi Province; the Longmen Grottoes in Luoyang, Henan Province; and the Guangyuan and Dazu grottoes in Sichuan Province. The statues in the grottoes are peerless in the world both in quantity and workmanship.

Many great projects of sculptural art were launched with the spread of Buddhism from the Northern Wei Dynasty (386-534) to the Sui and Tang dynasties (581-907). While the products of the early Northern Wei Dynasty still bore marks of foreign influence, Chinese style had become mature in the Tang Dynasty. The solemn Buddha sculptures applied with various colors had reached the unprecedentedly high artistic level, exhibiting the boldness of vision of the Chinese people. The colored sculptures in Dunhuang and Maijishan of Gansu Province were characterized by great originality, for it was difficult to carve on the local gravel. The Tang sculptures in Mogao Grottoes glowed with extraordinary splendor. Yang Huizhi, a famous expert of clay sculpture, had produced many statues in various temples. Many artists followed suit to produce a great number of clay sculptures in Buddhist temples, using a technique unique to Chinese Buddhist art.

The paintings carved on bricks and stones prospered in the Han Dynasty. Some colored murals were also found in Han tombs. Most of the Buddhist grottoes were decorated with murals since Buddhism was introduced to the interior of China along the Silk Road in Xinjiang. According to the *Chinese Civilization* by a French author, quite a few murals had been taken by Westerners, and preserved in European and American museums. The splendid murals in Mogao Grottoes in Dunhuang with their unique styles, represent the cream of China's national art.

Although influenced by foreign countries during the early stage, the murals in the Kirzil Grottoes of Xinjiang and those of the Northern Wei Dynasty in Mogao Grottoes vary in both content and technique when expressing the same subjects. Many of the Indian Buddhist murals in Ajanta Grottoes depict recreational activities, such as feasting and playing games. The Buddhas and other figures are splendidly decorated and brightly colored. Even subjects like "Subduing the Devils" were represented in a relaxing atmosphere, while the murals of the Northern Wei Dynasty in Dunhuang depict the stories of ascetic practices. For example, "Feeding a Person to a Tiger" makes one feel as terrified as if he were in the hell. It was probably due to the situation at that time—at the age of the ceaseless wars and slaughters, when the people were at a loss what to do to make their living, and the rulers tried to use religion to make the people obedient. Therefore, rough and strong lines and colors were applied in the paintings, which was an inevitable reflection in art of taking religion as a pragmatic tool.

The Sinicization of Buddhist art, which had started much earlier, was completed in China during the Sui and Tang dynasties. As early as the Liang Dynasty (502-557) in the Southern Dynasties period, Zhang Sengyao, a painter good at painting the images of Buddha, created new styles, taking the lead in the great development of the Sinicization of Buddhist images. Zhang Sengyao had exerted an enormous influence in the later stage of the Southern and Northern Dynasties, and many people studied his painting school—depicting the images of Buddha with succinct painting techniques.

The Buddhist paintings of Cao Zhongda were in high repute in the

Northern Dynasties period (386-534). Cao Zhongda being a native of the State of Cao in Central Asia, his paintings were characterized by the style of the Western Regions. Having stayed in the Central Plains for a long time, he had gradually developed his art the Chinese way, making it one of the four popular styles of the Tang Dynasty. In his paintings, the clothes of the figures were so close-fitting as if they were so wet as to cling to the skin—a style on the order of that of the Gupta Sculpture of India. In this respect, he was on a par with Wu Daozi—"Cao's wet clothes and Wu's floating ribbons," as contemporary critics put it. In Wu Daozi's works, the figures wore wide ribbons with ethereal lightness, which could be found in Dunhuang murals.

The murals of the Sui and Tang dynasties can be seen in the Maijishan and Mogao grottoes. Those of the Tang Dynasty in Dunhuang are extraordinarily rich in content, bright in color, and dignified and gorgeous in character modelling, depicting healthy and handsome male and female figures, usually ranking officials and palace ladies. The characters are depicted with elegant postures in the paintings, playing stringed and wind instruments before Buddha, in a way even more attractive than those in Ajanta murals. The images of donors in front of the Buddha include those of princes and officials of the same size as the images of the Buddha. The murals present the happy life in paradise and the quest for pleasures, in striking contrast to ascetic practices and mortification. The Buddhas, Bodhisattvas, celestials and heavenly warriors in the paintings are embodiments of beauty and health, which are completely identical to the social life and worldly feelings and wishes of the Tang Dynasty. The Buddhist paintings of the period are also embellished with many small views of the social life of the time, integrating the divine world with the mortal world, and with the feelings and wishes of the common people, thereby striking a responsive chord in the hearts of the masses. Moreover, Buddhist temples were not only places of worship, but they are also amusement centers.

The Chan sect was established in China as a school of Buddhist philosophy, advocating enlightenment rather than mortification, artistically stressing personality without sticking to one pattern. As a result, traditional Chinese freehand painting took on a completely new look.

Buddhism had not only exerted wide influence in Chinese literature and art, but also directly integrated with the Chinese society to take on a Chinese physiognomy. Different from the original Buddhism of Nepal and India, Chinese Buddhism has assimilated the achievements of Chinese culture. The Chinese part is the richest of all in the world's Buddhist trove. It is the cultural wealth of the Chinese people, containing their wisdom and labor.

(by Chang Renxia)

The Lord Guan Culture and
Lord Guan Temple

Guan Yu (160-219), a general of the State of Shu in the Three Kingdoms period (220-280), was the luckiest of all the Chinese military officers of the past dynasties. He rose from "a mere soldier of Shanxi" to Lord Guan—venerated by the people as an embodiment of loyalty, righteousness, propriety and wisdom for well over 1,400 years.

Guan Yu, or Lord Guan.

According to historical records, there was indeed such a person called Guan Yu, who was born in Changping Village of modern Yuncheng City, Shanxi Province in the third year of the Yanxi reign period (A.D. 160) in the Eastern Han Dynasty. When he was young, he had trained hard to be adept in martial arts. His stature was imposing and his bearing awesome. As he had a long well-trimmed beard and ruddy cheeks, he was called "a handsome bearded man."

Offending influential officials when trying to help people in distress at the age of 19, Guan Yu took refuge in Zhuozhou in modern Hebei Province. He and Liu Bei and Zhang Fei pledged to join in brotherhood in a peach garden. In order of their age, Liu Bei was the eldest brother; Guan Yu, mediate; and Zhang Fei, youngest. As Liu Bei was a descendant of the imperial household of the Han Dynasty, Guan Yu and Zhang Fei took him as their master. The three brothers pledged themselves to live and die together. Guan Yu had followed Liu Bei to go on expeditions everywhere since then. In the winter of the 24th year (219) of the Jian'an reign period, Guan Yu, due to carelessness in battle, was captured by soldiers of the State of Wu, and killed.

People had regarded Guan Yu as the greatest hero in the world from the Three Kingdoms to the Sui and Tang dynasties period. He has been worshipped as a deity since the Sui Dynasty. According to historical records, when propagating Buddhism at Dangyang in Hubei, Zhi Yi, an eminent monk of the Sui Dynasty, saw an immortal with a long beard one night, who claimed himself to be a general of the State of Shu, named Guan Yu, and now the owner of Dangyang Mountain, and he expressed his wish to become a Buddhist disciple. Zhi Yi memorialized it to Prince of Jin, who granted Guan Yu the title of Samgharama (Protect of the Dharma). The story had become very popular especially among the Song people, and Lord Guan temples mushroomed throughout the country. With the appearance of the full-length historical novel *Three Kingdoms* at the end of the Yuan Dynasty, his reputation was greatly boosted among people of all ages. The emperors of later periods all regarded Guan Yu as an embodiment of valor and loyalty, and as the guardian god of the royal families. A total of 16 emperors had granted Guan Yu honorific titles.

Tens of thousands of Guan Yu temples and statues had been erected throughout China since the Sui and Tang dynasties, especially in the Ming and Qing dynasties. Among the existing Lord Guan temples, the most famous include the ones in Dangyang of Hubei, Luoyang of Henan, Xiezhou of Shanxi, Guan Yu's home village in Yuncheng of Shanxi, and Dongshan Island of Fujian.

The Lord Guan Temple in Dangyang is situated at the foot of the Changbanpo Hill, an ancient battlefield and the burial place of the great general. Worshippers from Hong Kong, Taiwan and overseas like to go there to visit the resplendent and magnificent temple with red walls and yellow tiles. The ancient tomb of Lord Guan was some three meters in height, and over 60 meters in girth. The ancient trees on its top tower to the sky, its shade blotting out the sun. A passageway leads to the vault of the tomb, where an iron coffin is hung on iron chains, with altar lamps burning day and night and some other sacrificial utensils on its both sides. The passageway is now sealed to prevent robbery of the grave. At present, people can only visit the tomb and offer incense to Guan Yu in front of his tomb.

Going northward along the Jiaozuo-Liuzhou Railway from Dangyang, one reaches Guan Forest in Luoyang, Henan Province. In feudal Chinese society, the graves of the common people were called tombs, while those of sages, forests. Therefore, the burial place of Guan Yu's head was named "Guan Forest." Entering it, one sees a great array of couplets and inscribed boards, and the lifelike image of Lord Guan. Over 500 precious carved stone tablets dating from the Eastern Han and other dynasties were displayed in the eastern and western corridors, re-creating the ancient civilization of Luoyang—the former capital of nine dynasties.

The magnificent Lord Guan Temple in Xiezhou of Shanxi Province was erected in the ninth year (589) of the Kaihuang reign period of the Sui Dynasty, which was worshipped as the "number one temple of martial valor."

Situated 10 kilometers to the east of the Lord Guan Temple in Xiezhou, Changping Village, supposedly the home village of Lord Guan, were an ancestral tomb and temple dedicated to the celebrated warrior. Here, there is a nationally unique Goddess Hu Memorial Hall in memory of Guan Yu's wife, and also a hall in memory of Guan Yu's ancestors.

Lord Guan is enshrined and worshipped in every household on Dongshan Island in Fujian Province, off the southeastern coast. The Lord Guan Temple, washed by the sea, was built during the Hongwu reign period (1368-1399) of the Ming Dynasty, and is visited by worshippers every day.

The northernmost Lord Guan Temple is located in Hutou of Heilongjiang Province, facing the Russian city of Iman across the Wusuli River. During the reign period of Emperor Yongzheng (1723-1736) of the Qing Dynasty, a number of farmers from Jilin Province made a big fortune by digging medicinal herbs here by the Wusuli River. Thinking this was all due to Lord Guan, they contributed money to build a temple in his memory by the river to express their gratitude. This "pocket-size" temple with an area of only 82 square meters is now worshipped by the local people as the "symbol of ancient northeastern civilization."

Among the 116 Lord Guan temples of various sizes in Beijing built during the Ming and Qing dynasties, the one at Zhengyang Gate was the most famous, where great sacrificial ceremonies were held every year, and graced with the presence of emperor and his ministers. The imperial ceremonies of conferring honorific titles on Guan Yu were also held there. Unfortunately, however, those temples have all gone out of existence. To recover the historical relics, a baldachin has been erected in Yonghegong Lamasery, where an image of Lord Guan is enshrined. It is reported that Lord Guan temples of various sizes in Taiwan now total more than 460, and more under construction. One of the outstanding examples is the temple enshrining and worshipping Guan Yu in Tainan, which was first built during the Wanli reign period of the Ming Dynasty, and has been designated as one of the 16 "first-grade historical sites" in Taiwan. The new sculpture of Lord Guan in Putian Palace in Xinzhu County is 50 meters high together with the seat. Other famous temples include the Xingtian Palace in Taibei, Wenheng Hall in Gaoxiong, Shengshou Palace in Taizhong, Xietian Palace in Yilan, and Wenwu Temple in Sun and Moon Lake. On Lord Guan's birthday lively activities are held in the temples, attracting crowds of pilgrims.

Since the 1980s, funds have been raised to protect historical sites in some areas of the Chinese mainland. Dilapidated temples have been rebuilt, statues re-decorated, new tablets erected, and new couplets carved. The famous temples in Luoyang, Dangyang, Dongshan, Hutou and Xuchang have been restored to their original condition in recent years.

Lord Guan was not only venerated by emperors as a loyal and righteous sage, but also worshipped by the common people as a "universal god" who could wipe out pests and diseases, drive out evil spirits, bring in wealth and treasures, and protect businessmen. Today, statues of Lord Guan are enshrined and worshipped by people mainly in their homes, shops, companies and restaurants, and even in bars and top-grade karaoke halls in south China.

It was a popular practice to ask gods for an oracle in the old days. For example, the Lord Guan Temple at Zhengyang Gate in Beijing was always crowded with visitors who came to pray and draw "divination sticks of Lord Guan." The practice is still observed in some areas nowadays. For example, a continuous stream of visitors still come to the Lord Guan Temple on Dongshan Island in Fujian Province to consult the oracle, either praying for Lord Guan's blessing or "prophesy" on various problems— such as whether they can go to sea the next day, if their boyfriends or girlfriends are good, or when the roof beam of a house being built should be installed. With the booming of tourism, the practice has become a recreational activity for some tourists.

Temple fairs are an extension of the Lord Guan culture. They are held on Guan Yu's birthday, at which sacrifices are offered, and goods are traded. A "living Lord Guan" would come on stage to give a performance on large-scale art festivals. At present, scores of traditional opera routines are associated with Lord Guan, especially the red-face one in Peking opera is very popular among the masses. With the development of tourism, more and more varieties of the images of Lord Guan have been elaborately produced out of copper, silver, jade, sandalwood, painting brush, knife and scissors.

(by Zhu Zhengming)

A General View of Traditional Chinese Medicine

A treasure of Chinese culture, traditional Chinese medicine (TCM) is a unique supplement to modern medicine and healthcare in China. It plays a role that is irreplaceable by Western medicine in prevention and treatment of diseases.

TCM and Ancient Chinese Culture

Ancient Chinese culture and TCM originate from the same source. A Chinese legend from primitive times claims that Shen Nong tasted various herbs in his discovery of medicine. *Shen Nong's Herbal Classic*, written in the late Eastern Han Dynasty (25-220 A.D.), is China's earliest extant pharmaceutical work. *The Internal Canon of Medicine*, China's earliest medical book, is a summary of medical theories in ancient China.

Bian Que, also known as Qin Yueren, was a prominent doctor in the Warring States Period (475-221 B.C.). *The Classic on Medical Problems*, a medical work handed down to today, was attributed to him, but it is actually a collection of his medical theories compiled by his followers later according to oral teachings.

Hua Tuo was a very famous doctor during the late Han Dynasty, but his methods of treatment are long lost. Medical books bearing his name were actually written by others under his name. Afterward, Zhang Zhongjing wrote a complete book of medical formulary and started formal teaching in medicine.

During the Sui Dynasty (581-618), the imperial physician, Chao Yuanfang, and his team compiled the 50-volume *Treatise on the Causes and Symptoms of Diseases*. Finished in 610, it focused on causes and symptoms of diseases rather than providing prescriptions.

During the Northern Song Dynasty (960-1127), two voluminous medical works were collectively compiled: *Peaceful Holy Benevolent Prescriptions* and *General Collection for Holy Relief*. The latter, comprehensive and much more detailed, was based on the former at the behest of Emperor Huizong during the last years of the Northern Song Dynasty.

The Jin and Yuan dynasties (12th-14th centuries) saw epidemics caused by frequent wars. Doctors of different schools adopted different ancient medical works and combined them with their respective experience. Thus the "Four Major Medical Schools of the Jin and Yuan Dynasties" were formed.

In the Ming Dynasty (1368-1644), physician and pharmacist Li Shizhen had spent 27 years traveling the greater part of the country, gathering medicinal herbs, collecting folk remedies, visiting folk physicians, woodcutters, medicinal herb farmers and people of other walks of life, before finally completing the great pharmaceutical work, *Compendium of Materia Medica*. This work is a comprehensive summary of achievements of Chinese pharmacy before the 16th century and an outstanding contribution to world pharmacology.

Many comprehensive medical books appeared during the Qing Dynasty (1644-1911), together with many shorter works that were convenient for reference. These books further enriched the theoretical system and practical experience of traditional Chinese medical science and pharmacology.

Since the foundation of the People's Republic of China, the government has paid great attention to inheriting and developing the heritage of traditional Chinese medical science and pharmacology. In 1955, the Ministry of Health set up the Academy of Traditional Chinese Medicine, thus enabling TCM to develop more systematically and thoroughly.

The Analytical Treatment of TCM

TCM emphasizes analytical treatment. Just as the term implies, the doctor plans treatment according to diagnosis based on overall analysis of symptoms and signs, before deciding on the therapy and medication. The diagnosis is given after analysis, and the treatment after further deliberation.

The doctor comes to a diagnosis according to the symptoms, which include changes in the patient's tongue, complexion, and pulse condition. Based on the TCM theories on physiology, pathology, etiology and pathogenesis, the doctor identifies the cause, location, seriousness and condition of a disease by observing the changes in the patient's symptoms and signs. Causes include wind, chill, heat, dampness, dryness, intoxication, parasite, food, indigestion and stasis. Locations include Yin-Yang, internal organs, main and collateral channels, Qi (vital energy), blood, exterior and interior. The degree of seriousness can be shallow or deep, light or heavy, and tendency to get better or worse. The condition of a disease can be new or chronic, mild or serious, critical or not critical. The doctor needs to identify the principal and secondary aspects of a disease and its degree of urgency, before choosing among the eight treating methods, which include diaphoresis, emetic therapy, purgation, mediation, warming, heat-clearing, resolving, and tonification. According to the method, the doctor prescribes for the patient, choosing effective medication for the disease, and giving directions about the dosage and decocting method. The process of analytic treatment consists of examining, diagnosing, and treating. Correct diagnosis and medication are essential to achieve the best curative effect.

Although there are unchanging laws in analytic treatment, the treatment is very flexible, conforming to specific patient and disease in a specific time, place and climate. It is a treatment that combines theory and practice, focusing on the character of the specific disease while conforming to the patient's age and physique, as well as changes in the patient's condition. The aim of the treatment is recovering the original physical balance and harmony that was disturbed by the disease.

Analytic treatment emphasizes high specialization. Like cutting the dress according to the figure, the treatment is given according to the specific patient, time, place and symptom.

For example, cold patients may have the same symptoms, such as headache, runny nose, pain, and fever, but according to TCM, they should not be treated with the same medication. The cause, feature, and type of the cold should be identified before the treatment is given. There are always differences from patient to patient. Some patients have a yellow, thick nasal discharge and feel thirsty; some have a clear nasal discharge and are not thirsty; some feel tired, weak and short of breath. So the doctor gives different treatments and medication according to the different symptoms. A treatment that follows the principles of analytic treatment achieves the desired curative effect. Otherwise, instead of curing the patient, the treatment will aggravate the disease, even causing harm to the patient.

An ancient story goes: Once there was a doctor whose son happened to have a fever. Having examined him, the doctor concluded that White Tiger Decoction (ingredients: plaster, rhizoma anemarrhenae, rice, and licorice) should be used. But he feared that this strong decoction, with its pungent flavor and cool nature, might cause some side-effects on his son. Hesitating, he murmured to himself: "I'd use White Tiger Decoction if he weren't my own son." His apprentice overheard this, unbeknownst to the doctor. The doctor then decided to use another decoction and told his apprentice to prepare it. The doctor's wife heard from the apprentice what the doctor had murmured to himself, and insisted that he prepare the White Tiger Decoction—without her husband's knowledge. The son's fever abated after he took the White Tiger Decoction, and the doctor did not suspect anything until his wife told him the truth. From this, the doctor learned the lesson that treatment should only be given in accordance with the patient's real condition. With this example, it is illustrated that objectivity is most important in analytic treatment. The doctor must not be affected by personal feelings. The more objective the diagnosis is, the more effective the cure will be.

The spirit of analytic treatment permeates the development history of TCM. It is the general principle that is followed in such TCM divisions as internal medicine, surgery, gynecology, pediatrics, acupuncture and moxibustion, and massage treatment.

Using Ancient Medical Method to Treat Today's Diseases

TCM has distinguished itself in clinical practice with its curative powers. Its marvelous effects have been noted in modern scientific evaluations. The curative principles of drug and non-drug therapies contain profound philosophy, practicality and an undoubted scientific basis.

Malaria is a very harmful acute contagious disease that occurs in

China and the other parts of the world, especially Southeast Asia and Africa. The ancient Chinese learned in fighting malaria about the powers of sweet wormwood, the root of antipyretic dichroa, and the root of Chinese thorowax. Combining that experience and modern science, today's scientists have extracted the essence of sweet wormwood, which has excellent effects against malignant malaria and *P. Falciparum* infections that occur in areas with chloroquine protozoa, saving many lives. The World Health Organization has lavished praise for the unique structure and new functions of these medications.

To treat patients with HBV, Chinese doctors strengthen their toxic resistance and immune system by clearing heat and expelling dampness, promoting blood circulation and removing blood stasis, and strengthening body resistance. A recent clinical effectiveness rate was 86.3%, the rate of liver function recovery was 87.3%, and the relapse rate of HAA is 30%. A preparation for reducing aminopherase, developed with the fruit of the Chinese magnolia vine, has won an international gold prize.

TCM has achieved a new level in the prevention and treatment of common cardiovascular and cerebrovascular diseases, which are the most harmful to human health and the most widespread. According to Professor Weng Xinzhi, a famous Chinese medical scientist, the 400-odd in-patients with acute myocardial infarction in the hospital where he works were randomly divided into two groups. One group were treated with Western medicine only, and the other group were treated with the combination of the same Western medicine and the "anti-myocardial infarction mixture" developed by the Academy of Traditional Chinese Medicine according to "treating principles of activating blood circulation and supplementing Qi." It proved that the latter group had a lower incidence of complications and a lower death rate than the former group. TCM also has produced benefits in treating angina pectoris and high blood pressure. Scalp acupuncture has drawn international attention as a therapy for treating hemiplegic paralysis.

Based on rheum officinale's effects of "invigorating hollow organs," "removing blood stasis and helping production of new tissues," and experience from ancient times, Chinese doctors used various preparations containing rheum officinale to treat patients with chronic renal failure, and have found that they can improve patients' conditions by stopping the over-decomposition of the proteins in the organism and helping the excretion of the metabolized wastes in the blood such as urea nitrogen and creatinine through defecation or urination.

The Great Semen Cuscutae Drink, containing extractions from the seed of Chinese dodder, *Fructus ligustri lucidi*, *Eclipta prostrata*, *Psoralea corylifolia* and fleece-flower root, is used to treat blood cancer. A clinical trial showed that 13.6% of 169 patients were basically cured, and 33.7% improved. Extractions from *Indigo naturalis* and *Securinega suffruticosa* are effective in treating chronic myeloid leukemia.

It has been discovered that TCM can be used to treat patients with malignant tumors. It can improve the patients' living quality and reduce their side-effects from radiotherapy and chemotherapy. 103 patients with third-stage gastric cancer were treated with chemotherapy and Chinese medication for strengthening the spleen and tonifying the kidney after operation. As a result, their survival rate increased. 102 of the 103 patients (99.3 percent) lived one more year, 54 of 68 patients (79.41 percent) lived three more years and 26 of 47 patients (55.32 percent) lived five more years.

Based on the TCM principle that "the acid is astringing, and the astringent solidifying," Chinese scientists developed from Chinese gall and alum the "Xiao Zhi Ling" injection to treat piles, which has produced satisfactory effects on internal piles and the prolapse of the rectum. It won an international gold prize.

In the 1970s, TCM practitioners achieved excellent results in treating extensive (90 percent) burns by combining Chinese and Western medicine, among the most advanced in the world. In recent years, a "wet exposure" therapy was developed to treat less severe burns. This therapy enables the surface of the wound to heal in a short time and achieves a low infection rate and a better skin-grafting effect than the dry therapy, which keeps the surface of the wound dry while the scab is forming. The therapy has gained international attention.

Extrauterine pregnancy is an acute disease in obstetrics and gynecology. Based on the TCM theory of "promoting blood circulation and removing blood stasis," Chinese scientists achieved a breakthrough with a compound that contains the root of red-rooted salvia, root of common peony, peach kernel, *Curcuma zedoary*, etc. It helps remove the blood or hematomole in the abdomen, which has been confirmed by treatment and follow-up study of 600 cases and further by animal tests.

The artificial periodic therapy using Chinese medicine has produced satisfactory effects in treating infertility. According to TCM theory, "reproduction depends on the kidneys." Regulating the growth process of the ovarian follicle with a medication that tonifies kidney Yin and Yang has proved to produce effects in treating functional disturbances of the ovary and infertility. Among 154 cases of infertility caused by ovulation disfunction, the conception rate after treatment is 78.57% (121 cases).

Based on the principles of "equal importance of muscle and bone, treatment of internal and external, cooperation of doctor and patient, and combination of exercise and rest," bone fracture doctors have treated over 10,000 fracture patients by combining advantages of Chinese and Western medicine in treating bone fractures. Excepting patients with mental disorders, most patients are soon cured—a great development. Treatment of soft tissue injury using massage relaxes the muscles and improves blood circulation. It has won praise from patients from China and abroad for its immediate effect.

The clinical effects that TCM has achieved are the result of treatment theories and law instilled from practice. TCM stresses balance of the inner environment of the organism, unification and harmony of the inner and outer environments, and the law of life and treatment timing. It is important to analyze the illness and the patient's condition and to study the characteristics of the symptom. TCM emphasizes the relationship between internal organs, main and collateral channels and the body surface. Doctors' professional ethics are also important. The above have guaranteed the transmission of TCM through successive generations.

Although it originated from ancient times, TCM has been proven useful in modern times—"ancient prescriptions can be used to treat modern diseases." When modern science is applied to further explain the mechanism and theory of its curative effects, it will attract more attention.

(by Chen Keji)

The Magic of Acupuncture and Moxibustion

Acupuncture and moxibustion are traditional Chinese therapies that the ancient Chinese often used to prevent diseases and give emergency treatments. Besides all kinds of pain, they can also be used to treat internal, surgical, gynecological and pediatric diseases and all kinds of diseases occurring in the skin, mouth, eyes, ears, nose and throat. Requiring simple tools, acupuncture and moxibustion are easy to do and can be done anytime and anywhere. They can especially increase the rescue rate among emergency patients.

How can a small needle perform such magic? As early as 2,000 years ago, ancient doctors provided a perfect answer to the question. Ancient Chinese discovered that a human body consists of 11 internal organs, 5 sense organs, 9 apertures, 4 limbs, 100 bones, and skin, hair, veins and flesh. Qi, blood and body fluid are the material bases for the activities of the human body. The complicated main and collateral channels, through which Qi and blood flow, link the internal and external. They combine all parts of the human body into an integral whole, maintaining the human body's normal activities. Ancient Chinese also found that on the surface of the human body were acupoints, which were closely related to the internal organs and main and collateral channels. The acupoints transmit external stimulations to the internal organs and channels, affecting and adjusting their functions. The existence of acupoints for main and collateral channels as well as internal organs provides a sound material basis for the science of acupuncture. A disease is a result of a functional disturbance of one of the internal organs, a disorder of Qi, or an imbalance of Yin and Yang, which in turn is caused by various reasons. Stimulating relevant acupoints on the surface of the human body by way of acupuncture or moxibustion will adjust the function of the internal organ through the main and collateral channels, balance the Yin and Yang, enable Qi to flow freely upward and downward, improve the human body's immune system, and cure diseases. The theory that the acupoints are related to the internal organs has been proved by a large amount of clinical and laboratory research in modern times.

Using acupuncture and moxibustion to adjust the balance of Yin and Yang in the human body and affect the functions of the internal organs is obviously bi-directional. The therapies are superior to many other therapies because they produce quick results without causing side-effects or wounds.

Acupuncture and moxibustion are great inventions of the Chinese nation. They have a long history. At first they were only standard methods of treatment in ancient Chinese medicine. It was two millennia ago that they became a special branch of clinical medicine, which contains basic theories on main and collateral channels and acupoints, methods of acupuncture and moxibustion, and clinical experience in treating various diseases.

The earliest application of acupuncture and moxibustion dates back to remote antiquity. At that time, coarse tools of production, such as scrapers and pointed stone tools, were often used to let blood and reduce swelling. Later, a special tool for acupuncture—the stone needle—came into being and was used until the Iron Age, when it was replaced by the iron needle. One of the Han Dynasty stone reliefs from the second century depicts acupuncture with a stone needle. A half-man, half-bird divine creature is pushing a stone needle into the body of a patient. This is a scene of early acupuncture therapy with a stone needle. Medical literature of later ages included theories and experience of acupuncture and moxibustion. According to statistics, over 300 ancient Chinese medical books on acupuncture and moxibustion have been handed down to posterity.

In recent times, acupuncture and moxibustion have developed rapidly, and a modern acupuncture and moxibustion system with stimulation of acupoints as the basis is fast taking shape worldwide. Various types of equipment for and methods of acupuncture and moxibustion have been developed and used. Diagnosis through acupoints is also becoming popular. With modern technology, scientists have made great progress in explaining the principles of acupuncture and moxibustion, the nature of main and collateral channels, and acupuncture anesthesia. It is clear that with future scientific discoveries about main and collateral channels, Chinese acupuncture and moxibustion will make even more contributions to human health.

The acupuncture and moxibustion craze that has swept the world in recent years is still growing. In 1975, at the request of the World Health Organization, international acupuncture and moxibustion training centers were set up in Beijing, Shanghai, and Nanjing. These centers have trained several thousand practitioners from over 100 countries. At present, acupuncture and moxibustion have spread around the world. More and more schools and institutions specializing in acupuncture and moxibustion have been established in many countries, and many Chinese experts in this field have been invited to teach in those countries.

(by Tian Conghuo)

Qigong Breathing Exercise

Qigong (breathing exercise) is an integral part of TCM. It is commonly accepted in China that Qigong can be used to treat diseases. A patient can treat himself or herself by practicing Qigong, and a doctor can treat a patient by directing Qi to him or her. Simple types of Qigong have just a few movements, so that it can be practiced by anyone, anywhere, while advanced kinds have complicated movements, giving the practitioner a more subtle treatment. It is estimated that there are millions of people practicing various kinds of therapeutic or health-preserving Qigong, and many more in other countries are starting to practice Qigong. Chinese Qigong masters are teaching in many countries and regions, and Chinese books and magazines on Qigong have been translated into many foreign languages.

History and Theoretical Basis

Chinese Qigong has a long history. According to historical records, as early as the 21st century B.C., Chinese people knew how to use Qigong in treating arthritis with fixed pain caused by dampness. There are pictographic characters meaning "treatment with Qigong" in inscriptions on bones and tortoise shells of the Xia and Shang dynasties. After the Zhou Dynasty, practicing methods of Qigong started to develop and people started to study the theory of Qigong. *The Book of Changes*, a philosophic classic of the Western Zhou Dynasty (11th century - eighth century B.C.) that has greatly influenced Chinese culture, set a theoretical foundation for Qigong with its theory of Taiji (quintessence of the universe) and Yin-Yang. During the Spring and Autumn and Warring States periods (eighth century - third century B.C.), philosophers of various schools discussed Qigong in their works. Up to the present, *Lao Zi*, a Taoist classic, and *The Yellow Emperor's Canon of Internal Medicine* are still regarded as classics of Qigong theory. During those periods, Qigong masters developed many ways to practice Qigong based on their own experience. Later, treatises on maintaining good health by practicing Qigong were published, and the complete, systematic Chinese Qigong science was gradually formed. With Taoist theory and practice as the major part, it combines the essence of health-keeping theories and practice of medical, Confucian and Buddhist schools. According to statistics, so far, there are nearly 1, 000 known methods of practicing Qigong. Although some people have doubts about or even attack Qigong, and some Qigong masters are charlatans, the curative effects of Qigong and its value in research on the human body are beyond doubt.

The doctrine of Qigong is deeply rooted in traditional Chinese culture. According to Lao Zi, "The Tao gives birth to the One, the One gives birth to the Two, the Two give birth to the Three, and the Three give birth to the ten thousand creatures (i.e., all creatures). The ten thousand creatures have Yin and Yang as their components. The joining together of Yin and Yang brings harmony." The One means the primal fluid of the cosmos, or Taiji; the Two means the Yin and Yang deriving from Taiji; and the interaction between Yin and Yang and their movements give birth to all creatures. This is the Taiji model that ancient Chinese philosophers used to describe the unity of the cosmos. Heaven and Earth are Taiji on a large scale, and the human body is Taiji on a small scale. Everything in the world follows the law of Taiji and Yin and Yang. This concept of unity and harmony and the Way of Nature or "unity of Heaven and mankind" form the theoretical basis for the science of Qigong. The different schools of Qigong are common in their basic principles, which are adjusting thought, breath and body to achieve unity of vital essence, energy and spirit, unity of man and Nature, and the best state of life. In this way, disease is cured without medical treatment, the elderly become healthy, and the healthy become stronger.

Static Exercises and Dynamic Exercises

Chinese Qigong practices can be divided into static exercises and dynamic exercises, but the two are often difficult to tell apart because exercises frequently combine both. Recently, Qigong practices have been divided into five schools according to their characteristics, purposes, and requirements:

1. The breathing school, which focuses on training exhalation and inhalation.
2. The Daoyin school, which combines physical exercises with controlled breathing.
3. The meditation school, which regulates mental activities and tranquilizes the mind. It includes most static exercises.
4. The mind-concentration school, which requires the practitioner to focus his or her mind on a certain portion within the body with eyelids drooping.
5. The Qi cycling school, which conducts Qi to circulate through all the channels and collaterals in the body.

The method of treating diseases by sending Qi to the patient without touching him or her is not part of any of the above schools. Based on static and dynamic exercises, it is done by concentrating the mind on a certain acupoint and sending Qi to it. During the treatment, the Qigong master affects the patient with his or her Qi, nourishing the patient's vital energy, expelling the pathogen, and balancing Yin and Yang. The method is convenient, effective and practical; it is becoming a new school of Qigong.

Essentials of Qigong

Qigong is a way of training oneself by making use of one's subjective initiative, a technique unique to the humanity. Therefore, it is very important for the practitioner to correctly conduct himself or herself according to his or her own subtle feelings, or there is a danger of harming oneself. The Chinese Qigong community has summarized four essentials that apply to the various schools of Qigong.

Remaining relaxed, calm and natural, astringing the mind and Qi

Being calm, relaxed and comfortable, one can quickly get into a Qigong state, with the mind keen and Qi flowing smoothly. With the eyes, ears, nose, tongue and body astringed, the practitioner stops any distracting thoughts, concentrates his or her mind and feels the conditions within his or her body.

Soft breathing and combination of the mind and Qi

A practitioner should not get impetuous, but should breath softly and deeply like a newborn baby, concentrate the mind lightly, and keep the body relaxed but not slack. The mind should guide the flow of Qi, but not force it, until the mind and the vital energy become integrated, or else the Qi will get stagnant or out of control.

Keeping a straight body and integration of movements and mind

The practitioner should stand straight, with head and neck upright, chin drawn slightly inward, chest relaxed, back straight, shoulders and elbows down loosely, waist relaxed, buttocks drawn inward, knees bent slightly and feet pointing forward. Such a post holds inner strength. The waist should be the axis of any movement. The upper body should move lightly, while the lower body should move with force. The movement of the whole body should be coordinated. The eyes should move with the hands, waist and feet so as to integrate the mind and the physical movements; thus the essence of life produces Qi, and Qi in turn produces the mind.

Fixed exercise and appropriate time of practice

Practicing Qigong is a process of forming conditioned reflex. A practitioner should do a certain kind of exercise instead of different, contradictory kinds. Practicing at a proper time will enhance the effect. A beginner can practice for 20 to 40 minutes at one time, and prolong the practice when he or she gets more used to the exercise. The time length can be decided according to the time when the effect is produced and the practitioner does not feel tired.

During the practice, as the mind is concentrated on the inside of the body, the practitioner will find his or her senses keener, and may have mild hallucinations, such as feeling the flow of water or seeing images. That is a normal phenomenon, and the practitioner should not become excited and try to seek it or get frightened and try to avoid it, but should let it appear and disappear by itself.

Probing the Mysteries of Wushu Martial Arts

Chinese Wushu (Kungfu or martial arts), with a history of several millennia, has developed on the nourishment of traditional Chinese culture. In spite of many bans on it and suppression by feudal rulers, it has thrived among the common people instead of dying out. This evinces the strong attraction and vitality of Wushu in China. The present Wushu of different schools and styles embodies the wisdom and culture of all the ethnic groups in China throughout history.

Beginning and Development

The initial form of Wushu appeared during prehistoric times, when the people fought against Nature, hunting for food and clothing, and guarding against attacks by animals and natural disasters.

In slave and feudal societies, weapons and military techniques provided ideal conditions for the development of Wushu in an environment of frequent wars between tribes and states. For quite a long period, Wushu was meant for actual combat.

People needed Wushu to fight enemies in slave society. They worked in the fields during spring, summer, and autumn while teaching and learning Wushu in winter. This primitive military art influenced the Wushu of later generations.

In the Spring and Autumn and Warring States periods (770-221 B.C.), rulers of different states promoted Wushu. In the Spring and Autumn Period, Wushu masters gathered together in the spring and autumn of each year for competition and mutual exchange. At that time, the standard was two-person combat, while solo exercises were meant as training for two-person fights. The latter developed into Wushu movements.

In the Qin Dynasty (221-206 B.C.), there appeared Wushu movements for two people.

Influenced by the Qin Dynasty, during the Han Dynasty (206 B.C.-220 A.D.), Wushu movements further developed in both form and content. There appeared boxing imitating animal movements. In that period, Wushu started to be regarded as an art with characteristics of sport and various techniques and styles.

The system of military examinations started in the Tang Dynasty (618-907 A.D.). Standards were set for selecting warriors, and prizes and honors were given to encourage people to practice Wushu.

In the Song Dynasty (960-1279), many people practiced Wushu to defend themselves against foreign invaders. The government set up Wushu schools and hired masters of military strategy and Wushu as teachers. There appeared many non-governmental Wushu organizations. During that time, many series of Wushu movements were standardized, with starting and ending movements and courtesies with hands.

In the early Qing Dynasty (1644-1911), Wushu was banned among the common people, but spread in secret Wushu organizations. There were many boxing styles in the Qing Dynasty, with scores of major styles and hundreds of series of boxing movements.

After 1949, when the People's Republic of China was founded, Wushu developed in a healthy, all-around way, and was appointed one of the events in sports competition. A national Wushu organization—the China Martial Arts Association—was founded, and Wushu became more and more systematic, scientific, and

Gongsun Daniang practicing the art of fencing.

41

standardized. Chinese Wushu delegations and instructors have been sent to other countries. More and more people from other parts of the world are learning Wushu in China. In addition, various international exchanges on Wushu have been held. Chinese Wushu has become popular around the world.

Wushu and Philosophy

In its history, Wushu absorbed ancient Chinese philosophic principles, as demonstrated by the names of various types of boxing, such as Taiji (supreme ultimate) Quan, Bagua (eight diagrams) Zhang, Baji (eight extremities) Quan and Xingyi (form-and-will) Quan. The ancient Chinese philosophical theory that "man is an integral part of nature" also influenced Wushu. As Zhuang Zi, an ancient Chinese philosopher, said, "Heaven and Earth coexist with me, and I am one with all creatures." According to the theory, Wushu masters believe that there is an intrinsic link between humanity and the universe, and that one cannot achieve the aim of practicing Wushu unless one achieves harmony with the universe. Therefore, Wushu theory contains unification of internal and external exercises, emphasizing enhancement of practical effect by adapting oneself to changes in the universe and by using the effect of the environment on the human body. In ancient times, people chose to practice Wushu in wooded mountains, scenic places, or clean places at home, or to perform different exercises in different seasons. These all embody the theories of integration of Nature and humanity and of the subject following the object.

The Book of Changes, the oldest Chinese philosophical work, argues dialectically that "balance of Yin and Yang is the Way." Wushu masters believe that "balance of Yin and Yang is perfect practice," which gives rise to a series of Wushu concepts of correspondence of Yin and Yang, such as the dynamic and static, the firm and soft, the void and solid, and form and spirit. Ancient Chinese philosophical theories on the eight diagrams, five elements and quintessence of the universe are reflected in Wushu. Therefore Wushu has greater philosophic influence than other sports.

Using a short-hilted broad sword.

Wushu and Moral Character Cultivation

Since ancient times, Wushu practitioners have upheld the proverbs: "Morality is better than strength" and "Moral education comes before Wushu training." Almost all of the Wushu schools in the past put morality first.

Traditional Wushu morality includes patriotism, uprightness, politeness and faith. In old times, the Wushu community followed strict regulations and commandments. For example, each school had strict requirements about teaching disciples. The regulations of Shaolin Temple included: "Disciples should be selected with great care, and Wushu shall only be taught to those have proved to be honest and upright." The Wudang School also had five rules on admitting disciples; a low-quality, insidious, or bellicose person or one who indulged in excessive drinking would be turned down. Wudang rules also forbade adultery, theft, viciousness, obscenity, and gambling.

Because Wushu's very nature is founded on attack and defense, the slightest neglect of moral discipline can result in injury or even death. In ancient times, the Wushu community forbade attacking a total of eight vital parts of the human body. Today, the modern Wushu community conducts competitions according to the requirements of modern sport, and

43

therefore has drawn up competition rules and moral requirements according to current standards, so as to re-emphasize Wushu morality.

Wushu and Aesthetics

Wushu is characterized not only by exterior beauty, found in postures, movements, and techniques, but also deep interior beauty, emphasizing "life essence, vital energy, and spirit," "form coupled with spirit," and "physical health and inner vitality." The concepts of "vital energy," "rhythm," "will" and "spirit" in Wushu theory, are identical to the categories of ancient Chinese aesthetics. Therefore, demonstration of the interior beauty of Wushu requires understanding of traditional Chinese culture in addition to self-cultivation.

Since King Wu's triumph over Zhou (the last emperor of the Shang Dynasty) was commemorated in the composition "Great Martial Music" in the 11th century B.C., Wushu has been involved in literary and artistic fields, such as music, dance, poetry, opera, fiction, and acrobatics. Ancient martial dances and music were vigorous and majestic in style. Melodies reflecting ancient battles, such as "Ambush on All Sides" and "The General's Command" are still famous and played by musicians today. The "Grand Martial Dance" and "Bow and Arrow Dance" combine ancient martial arts with dancing.

Xia ke (chivalrous swordsmen or gallant persons) were a social force as early as the Warring States Period. During the Han and Tang dynasties, *xia ke* were highly influential figures in society. The ancient historian Sima Qian's "Biographies of Roving Swordsmen" can be regarded as one of the earliest Wushu tales, or tales of roving knights. The late Tang Dynasty saw an upsurge in the creation of such tales, in which the chivalrous swordsmen embody the common people's desires to eliminate tyrants, bring peace to the people, and reform the state. Tales of roving knights had been popular for over 1,000 years and became a fad in the early 20th century. Today, in Chinese mainland, Hong Kong and Taiwan, creation of such tales continues unabated.

Although stories of roving knights often have much room for improvement, they are rare outside China as a category of literature, except for the knight literature of the Middle Ages in Europe. With the development of modern science and technology, Wushu movies and TV dramas have become very popular. Scenes of Wushu fighting in Chinese operas enjoy great popularity, especially the spectacular ones in Peking Opera.

Wushu and Peking Opera

In Chinese opera, the movements and personalities of characters are communicated through singing and dancing. Wushu not only provides fighting scenes for operas, but also influences the content of operas and tastes of the audience.

Many actors and actresses of Peking Opera, one of the most popular and influential forms of Chinese opera, are skilled at Wushu. Tan Xinpei, who combined traditional forms with contemporary additions, was once a bodyguard. He especially excelled in using broadsword, even a real sword, onstage. He added Shaolin broadsword techniques into his performance. Yang Xiaolou, who also learned martial arts, merged them with his dancing and other movements, showing the audience the beauty of Wushu.

Besides actors specializing in martial roles, Mei Lanfang and Cheng Yanqiu, famous male actors playing female roles, benefited from their daily Wushu practice. Mei Lanfang practiced Wushu every day, and his performance of "Lady Yu Dancing with a Sword," widely acclaimed as a masterpiece of art, contained movements borrowed from form-and-will boxing and Taiji boxing.

Cheng Yanqiu started learning Wushu as a child; during Japanese invasion he once

Using twin hooked swords.

45

beat seven or eight armed spies barehanded at the Beijing Qianmen Railroad Station. He used to be a Wushu teacher in Geneva, teaching foreign students Taiji boxing. More important, he combined Wushu in his dancing performances. Without his dexterity and skill in wielding the sword, he would not have been able to dance with his light, long silk sleeves with such grace.

Gai Jiaotian, an actor famous for playing heroes over his 60-year career, learned Wushu from a Kungfu master when he was young, to enhance his fighting performance and improve his appearance onstage. He believed that an actor's Wushu skills were like musical notes: an actor can create various stage images and express various feelings by selecting and arranging Wushu movements according to the plot, just like a musician composing a piece of music with each note expressing rich and complicated feelings. This remark of Gai Jiaotian perfectly fits the close relation between opera and dancing on one side and Chinese Wushu on the other.

(by Xu Cai and Liu Junxiang)

Fascinating Chinese Characters

Chinese is one of the four earliest written languages in the world, the others being ancient Egyptian, ancient Sumerian, and ancient Babylonian. Only Chinese is still used today.

From Drawings to Characters

Chinese characters are the written symbols of the Chinese language. In the long development of the language, ancient Chinese gradually developed Chinese characters from drawings. Drawings are a representation of things with lines, colors, and images. People expressed their knowledge, thoughts, and feelings through drawings. Drawing was a form of art entertainment during leisure as well as a means of communication between people. As time went by, people began to consciously use drawings to express themselves, thus developing drawn writing, the basis of Chinese characters.

Archeological finds reveal the process of drawings' development into today's characters. Since the 1930s, over 30 sites of ancient cultural relics have been discovered around China, dating from the Yangshao Culture (5,000 to 7,000 years ago) to the Shang Dynasty (ca. 16th century-11th century B.C.). Over 800 pottery relics have been unearthed, which are the direct and most reliable materials for studying the origin of Chinese characters.

Certain color pottery bowls unearthed from the Yangshao Culture ruins bear incised symbols varying in shape on the black outside rim. Those objects date back to 6,000 years ago. Some people believe that the symbols are primitive Chinese characters, because some of them are similar to characters from oracle bone inscriptions over 3,000 years ago. However, the similarity is likelier a coincidence, for most of the symbols are geometric figures, and look like signatures or clan emblems. The symbols are more like drawings than the earliest Chinese characters, though they might have had a certain influence on the formation of Chinese characters.

Four pictographic symbols were found on potteries from the late Dawenkou Culture 4,000 years ago. Obviously they are very different from the symbols mentioned above. The first symbol is like a *yue* battle-axe (an ancient weapon); the second looks like another kind of axe; the third looks like a sun above a flame or cloud, interpreted as "firelight" by some people and "morning" by others; the fourth consists of the third symbol and a symbol of mountain under it, believed to be a complex form of the third, or "firelight and mountain." The four symbols, believed to be clan names, are no longer simple pictures, but have some links with language. They are from the earliest stage of the development of Chinese characters.

Development of Chinese Characters

The primitive Chinese characters of Dawenkou Culture developed through over 1,000 years of collective contributions into the oracle bone inscriptions of 3,000 years ago, which was a relatively complete written language.

Evolved from drawings, primitive Chinese characters were pictographic, which was greatly limiting because there were shapeless things or very complicated and undistinguishable things. So methods of expressing ideas were needed. One of the symbols mentioned above is an ideograph because it combines two pictographic symbols. Such symbols broke the limitations of pictographs and represented a big step forward in the development of Chinese characters.

However, ideographs are still far from perfect, for language also reflects everything in the objective world with sounds. Many words cannot be written in ideographs. For example, we can use " 木 " to express the concept of "wood," but there are thousands of varieties of wood and trees, which cannot be distinguished with pictographs or ideographs, not to speak the mental activities: think, remember, forget, anger, hate, fear, etc. It was necessary for Chinese characters to develop from ideographic to phonetic.

There are two types of phonograms: one type only represents phonemes in speech, such as the alphabetic languages around the world; and the other represents both ideas and phonemes, such as Chinese characters since the oracle bone inscriptions.

Chinese characters, used to record words or morphemes as units of meaning, have one syllable each, and integrate symbols representing the shape, sound and meaning. The pictophonetic characters enables one to distinguish between homonyms. In the Han Dynasty (206 B.C.-220 A.D.), 80% of Chinese characters were pictophonetic, and today the proportion exceeds 90%. During the past 4,000 years, Chinese characters have developed from pictographic to ideographic and then to phonetic.

Formation of Chinese Characters

The formation of Chinese characters is very interesting. Its characteristics can be seen from the following ideographs.

Some ideographs are abstract or pictographic symbols. For example: —(one), 三 (three), 二 (under), 水 (water), 木 (wood), 禾 (corn), 象 (elephant) and 门 (door, gate).

Some ideographs consist of two or more pictographic symbols; some even representing a sentence. For example:

睡 (sleep): A man (亻) is sleeping on a mat (席) in a house (宀).

采 (pick): A pair of hands (爪) are picking fruits from a tree.

见 (see): The major part of the character is an eye (目), meaning "see."

森 (forest): "三" (three) meant "many" in ancient times, so three trees (森) means forest.

Change of Forms of Chinese Characters

Besides the general tendency of creating ideophonetic characters, the most obvious change in Chinese characters during the several millennia of development has been manifested in the form of writing. That is, changes in script have resulted in Chinese characters developing from pictograms into symbols consisting of a number of strokes. From oracle bone inscriptions to today's regular script, the form of Chinese characters has gone through two major changes: the first happened in the Qin (221-206 B.C.) and Han (206 B.C.-220 A.D.) dynasties when seal script developed into official script; the second took place in around the third century A.D. when official script was replaced by regular script, which has been used through the ages. Usually, *xiaozhuan* (lesser seal character), the script used nationally after Qinshihuang (First Emperor of Qin) unified China, and the scripts before it, are referred to as ancient Chinese scripts, including oracle bone inscriptions and inscriptions on bronze objects. The official script was the start of modern Chinese characters. The cursive hand is a simplified style of various scripts. The running hand is a commonly used handwriting style between the regular script and cursive hand.

Simplification of Chinese Characters

A written language must be convenient for writing. The writing styles and structures of Chinese characters have been simplified through the ages. Many simplified characters have been created throughout history. For example, today's "异" and "体" are simplified forms of "異" and "體". Simplification has been a general trend in the development of Chinese characters.

(by Guo Xiliang)

Tea and Teahouses

China being the home country of tea, tea production is a contribution of the Chinese nation to human civilization. Classics on tea, the tea ceremony and customs, tea sets and so on are all parts of traditional Chinese culture.

Lu Yu, respectfully called the "Saint of Tea," is always associated with tea in China. He lived more than a thousand years ago. He wrote *The Book of Tea*, a great work that tells how to pick, produce, brew, and drink tea.

The Book of Tea contains three *juan*.* The first *juan* deals with the origin of tea, its varieties and its properties. It also discusses 15 types of equipment for the processing of tea and the seven actual steps of the process, tea-gathering and tea-making requirements, and standards and principles of tea assessment. The second *juan* looks at the 25 utensils for

A tea set.

---

* A traditional thread-bound volume, usually containing a much shorter text than a volume in modern book publishing.

brewing and drinking, the principles of using these utensils, the correct ways of brewing and drinking tea, and the merits and demerits of different porcelain tea vessels in China. The third *juan* records curing tea, the water and firewood for brewing tea, the standards of drinking tea, the history of tea drinking and its taboos, the tea-producing areas, and the procedures and tools of tea making . Lu Yu writes, "Tea is a kind of bush that grows in the south. Its height ranges from one or two *chi** to dozens of *chi*. Large tea bushes that equal the span of a man's arms grow in mountains or valleys…." Lu Yu recorded the original seeds of tea bushes more than a thousand years before the British discovery of tea in India in 1823. In the book, Lu Yu tells stories about 42 well-known persons addicted to drinking tea and cites 48 different historical documents. The publication of *The Book of Tea* spread knowledge about tea and accelerated the popularization of tea drinking. Later, a *Supplement to "The Book of Tea"* was written. *The Book of Tea* has been translated into several languages and spread far and wide in many other countries. The Japanese tea ceremony, which is more elaborate and standardized than the Chinese, was evolved under the influence of Lu Yu's book.

For a long period of time, tea has become both a material drink and spiritual enjoyment. Pursuits associated with tea have also developed, such as tea-poetry writing, tea rites, tea ceremonies, tea parties, and tea feasts. Tea drinking has become both a culture and an art.

Tea drinking is beneficial to health, can cure diseases, and mould one's temperament. People should be familiar with tea-related knowledge, such as storing and brewing tea and the selection of tea vessels and the water for brewing, all of which embody the Chinese tea-drinking art.

Tea-drinking customs vary in China, some of which are briefly introduced in the following pages.

Gongfu Tea of Fujian and Guangdong Provinces

At the juncture of Fujian and Guangdong provinces, contiguous to the Taiwan Straits, are Dongshan Island in southern Fujian and Nan'ao

---

* *Chi* is a unit of length equaling one third of a meter.

Island in Guangdong. The local fishermen carry tea with them whenever they go to sea to fish or chat with friends. When a guest comes, the host or hostess will first get the tea-brewing stove going and, when tea is ready, chat with the guest over a cup of tea.

Careful tasting will demonstrate the quality of a tea. An old saying goes, "A professional knows the origin of a tea as soon as a sip of it is taken." After sipping the tea, one can tell whether it is "Xiaoxian" or "Dahongpao" from Mt. Wuyi of Fujian, or "Tieguanyin" or "Yizhichun" from Anxi of the same province.

Inhabitants of Dongshan and Nan'ao islands are very particular about tea-tasting. It needs time and skill to really taste the flavor of a tea. Hence the name, "Gongfu" tea, "gongfu" meaning "skill."

The Gongfu teaset includes three tiny cups, a boccaro teapot, a charcoal stove, and a kettle. Why three cups? A folk saying goes, "It's preferable to have three persons together sipping tea and tasting its flavor."

The teapot is just bigger than a walnut. It is only big enough to pour tea into three tiny cups for the persons to moisten their throats and distinguish the tea's color, fragrance and taste.

Time is another important factor. During the time it takes to drink the tea and appreciate its fragrance, the water in the kettle should boil once more and be poured twice. The hotter the tea is when drunk, the better it tastes. As the water should boil in a limited time, the kettle should contain one bowl of water only. Ten or twenty percent of the water should be left after every pouring, and then new water is added.

Charcoal is used as the fuel to eliminate odors and provide just the right temperature. The quality of the boccaro teapot directly affects the tea's color, fragrance, and taste.

"Sprout cultivation" was adopted to improve the quality of the tea brewed. The first round of tea brewed is poured into another bowl and poured back into the teapot after several rounds of drinking. After a long period of time, black-brown moss-like material (which is commonly called "tea sprout") accumulates on the inner walls of the teapot, and the longer the time passes, the thicker it grows. By using such a teapot, the tea is richer and more fragrant. Even when there are no tea leaves in the pot, the water brewed therein still smells fragrant.

When pouring water from the kettle into the teapot, one should hold the kettle high; when pouring the tea into the cups, one should keep the teapot low. In order for the tealeaves to be fully exposed to the water, one should pour boiling water around the rim of the teapot. When pouring tea, one should quickly pour the tea into the cups evenly to and fro, not one by one, which will make strength of the tea unequal. The drinker should not find tea dust in the cup. One should not finish a cup of tea but leave a little out of politeness; one should gently pour the remaining tea back onto the tea plate. The Gongfu tea ceremony is popular in south Fujian Province, and Chaozhou and Shantou in Guangdong Province, and also in Taiwan. It is also observed among Chinese in Southeast Asia.

Guangdong Teahouses

Teahouses and restaurants dominate the commercial areas of Guangzhou. It is said that Guangzhou is a good city to eat in because of the profusion of teahouses and restaurants. When Guangzhou residents meet, they often say, "Let's touch the bottoms of our teacups someday (i.e., to drink tea in a teahouse together)." There are many teahouses in small villages and towns in the suburbs. People go to teahouses mornings, middays or evenings. Teahouses are open from 4 a.m. into the small hours.

Guangzhou residents' tea-drinking habit has a long history. The city is the starting point of the tea trade route, from which Chinese tea seeds were transported, in 1780, to India, the largest tea producer in the world today. India began tea cultivation then. At that time, teahouses in Guangzhou were usually shabby. During the reign of Emperor Guangxu (1875-1908) of the Qing Dynasty, Sanyuan Teahouse, the first luxury teahouse in the city, appeared in the business center of Guangzhou. It was a gorgeously decorated four-storied building. Since that time, tea-rooms have been called teahouses, and tea-drinking is called "going to teahouses."

In their competition with each other, each teahouse tries to be different. They adopt different architectural styles. Some teahouses are built overlooking a pool like a stone boat; some are located in quiet and peaceful rockeries. They also try always to bring forth something new in their menus.

In the old days, the wealthy were guests in first-class teahouses, while common people went to ordinary ones, chatting over their teacups. If one pours tea for a friend, the latter lightly taps the table with two fingers as a token of gratitude. This custom stems from an old story. It was said that once when Emperor Qianlong (1736-1795) was traveling incognito to the south on a fact-finding tour, he poured tea for his servants, who bent two fingers on the table as a sign of curtesy, instead of kowtowing, which would otherwise betray the emperor's identity.

In the 1980s, great changes occurred in teahouses in Guangzhou. Some long-standing teahouses, such as Taotaoju, Beiyuan, and Panxi were re-decorated. Teahouses added food to broaden their business range, and some teahouses changed names to "restaurant."

Every morning, as soon as a teahouse's door is opened, frequent customers, primarily senior citizens, come and find their familiar seats. They enjoy drinking hot tea with two or more cookies and chatting with a few intimate friends.

Some people snatch a moment to go for a spell of afternoon tea. Evenings find lovers having a tête-à-tête over milk tea or lemonade.

Women now also go to these formerly typical male haunts. Many people prefer to hold wedding feasts, business meetings, or reunion parties at teahouses.

Chengdu Teahouses

The people of Sichuan are known for their frequenting teahouses. It is no exaggeration to say that teahouses in Sichuan are the best in China, and those in Chengdu are the best in Sichuan.

Chengdu residents are particular about comfort and atmosphere when drinking tea. The seats in teahouses are all comfortable chairs made of bamboo. The teaset includes three pieces: porcelain cup, porcelain lid, and metal saucer.

Teahouses in Chengdu have four notable characteristics: long history, large size, large number and high quality. Long history: *The Book of Tea* tells of "elderly Sichuan women selling tea and gruel," which shows that there were teahouses and tea booths over 1,000 years ago in Chengdu and other places in Sichuan. Large size: The Huahua Teahouse in Chengdu could accommodate more than 1,000 patrons at that time. Large number: There are as many as more than 600 houses now in Chengdu, about the same number as in the old days. High quality: This refers to quality service. A waiter named Pockmark Zhou in Jinchun Teahouse had a unique skill in serving tea. He carried a shiny copper kettle in his right hand and a pile of tin saucers and white porcelain teacups in his left hand. He raised his left hand and threw everyone a saucer on the table. He quickly put a teacup onto the saucer. The teacup was correctly laid before every customer. He poured water into each cup from one meter away without sprinkling a single drop. Finally, he stepped forward to cover each cup with its lid.

Chengdu has several time-honored teahouses, such as Chunlan Teahouse, Da'an Teahouse and Senyuan Teahouse. From their old decor and furniture one can get glimpses of local customs and practices.

Taoyuan's Leicha Tea

Taohuayuan in Taoyuan County, Hunan Province, is famous for its scenery and Leicha Tea.

Leicha Tea is made of ginger, tea leaves, sesame, rice and salt mixed with cooled boiled water and pounded into thick syrupy fluid with a hawthorn stick. Hence the name Leicha (Pounded Tea).

There are many rites for drinking Leicha. After the guests sit down at the table, the host or hostess places a small bowl with some Leicha in front of every guest and pours boiling water into the bowls to swirl. The kettle is held high off the table and the water is poured rapidly. The host or hostess sets the table with fried peanuts, fried soybeans, and so on beforehand to increase the tea's color, fragrance and taste.

Leicha has the functions of quenching thirst, promoting body fluid secretion, invigorating functioning of the stomach, lifting spirits, preventing common cold, and facilitating digestion. All year round, denizens of

Taohuayuan drink Leicha instead of eating lunch.

China's long history of tea production has also resulted in a wide spectrum of tea, such as green tea, black tea, oolong tea, scented tea, pressed tea, Baicha (a kind of unfermented or unbaked or unrolled tea, made by a special process), and yellow tea, to name a few. Other drinks with tea as the main ingredient have also been developed, such as bodybuilding tea, longevity tea, and quit-smoking tea.

Famous tea in China includes Longjing from West Lake (Zhejiang Province), Biluochun from Taihu Lake (Jiangsu Province), Maofeng from Mount Huangshan (Anhui Province), green tea from Wuyuan (Jiangxi Province), and Tieguanyin from Anxi (Fujian Province).

Tea drinking also depends on water quality, the tea utensils used, and the brewing method.

The relationship between water and tea is similar to that between water and wine. Lu Yu discusses tea water exhaustively in *The Book of Tea*: "Water from mountains is the best, river water is average, and well water is inferior."

Tea contains polyphenol materials. It turns brown black when exposed to molysite solution, and produces an astringent tasting "rust oil" when exposed to alkaline or chalybeate water. Soft water (less than 80 milligrams of calcium and magnesium ions per liter) is better for making tea; the tea brewed in this way is fragrant in flavor and bright in color. Generally speaking, spring water is the best, while water from rivers, lakes, and wells becomes soft water after settlement. City tap water should be kept in a jar for one night to increase the color, fragrance and taste of the tea.

The teaset includes a kettle, teapot and teacup. Nowadays, people have become more and more demanding of the teasets they use. The variety of teasets has also increased. Different types of teasets should be used for different types of tea. For example, glasses best preserve the color of quality green tea and scented tea, while porcelain cups are best for enhancing the fragrance of common green tea and scented tea. When making scented tea, a covered cup is best for keeping its fragrance.

Regarding brewing methods, first, water temperature is very important. The higher the water temperature, the more quickly the volatile material in tea water volatilizes. Usually, water at 80 degrees Celsius is best for making tea. Secondly, the amount of water should be appropriate. The ratio should be one glass of water to three grams of tea leaves. For the first brewing, between one-third and one-half of the water is appropriate. Using too much water will dilute the flavor. The second brewing should wait after several minutes. The third brewing comes after another few minutes. An old saying goes, "The first brewing yields only a mouthful of fragrance, the second brewing a strong flavor, the third brewing mellowness, and the fourth brewing no flavor."

(by Lin Yashun, Zhong Jian, Lu Bo, and Hong Zhou)

Alcoholic Drinks

More than 20 years ago, in Hebei Province, Chinese archeologists discovered two bronze wine casks in the tomb of the Prince of Zhongshan, dating back to 2,300 years ago. When the casks were opened, they were immediately struck by the smell of wine. One cask held 6.7 kilograms of a vivid green wine, and the other held three kilograms of a dark green wine.

These two containers of wine, along with jewelry, were funerary objects of the Prince of Zhongshan's tomb, and they show that wine occupied a high position in the colorful Chinese culinary culture. Various ancient wines, wine containers and paintings of drinking customs discovered in this and other tombs reveal a developing history of Chinese drinking with sharp epochal characteristics and China's rich and abundant wine culture.

Long History

Toward the end of the primitive society, surplus fruit or grain fermented itself with the passage of time and became "wine." Through experience and observation, people learned the process of fermentation and thus gradually learned to produce wine.

During the 1970s, archeologists excavating a site of Dawenkou Culture (a culture of the Neolithic Age, beginning about 4500 B.C.) in Shandong Province discovered large, strange-looking

A Shang Dynasty bronze *jia* – a round-mouthed three-legged wine vessel.

wine-making paraphernalia and realistic-looking pictures of the wine-making process. These pictures were all painted red, a mysterious noble color to people of the remote past. This discovery shows that about 7,000 years ago, winemaking in China had already reached a certain level.

During the Shang Dynasty (c. early 17th-11th century B.C.), China's wine culture was already highly developed. Many narrations about wine can be found in oracle inscriptions on tortoise shells and animal bones. People began to use sprouted grain to make wine, and there was a rich assortment of wine and wine utensils, complete with a suite of strict wine-drinking rites. With the application of distiller's yeast during the Zhou Dynasty (c. 11th century-256 B.C.), Chinese wine culture developed to a new stage.

Wine-making technique reached full maturity with the application of distillation equipment. Bai Juyi, a poet in the Tang Dynasty (618-907), mentioned "spirits" in one of his poems. The alcohol concentration was so high as to make them flammable. Spirits can be made only through distillation process. It can be seen that distillation had already been adopted during the Tang Dynasty.

In modern times, despite the introduction of new techniques in wine making in China, there are still three time-honored basic ways to make wine: by natural fermentation (particularly for fruit wine), by pressing (particularly for all types of yellow wine), and by distillation (particularly for all types of liquor or spirits).

Yellow wine (made of rice or millet) is a good representative example of Chinese wine culture. Yellow wine experts have suggested making yellow wine China's "national wine." This is because yellow wine has over 5,000 years of history, and its alcoholic content is not high, conforming to the modern trend toward drinking low-alcohol beverages. Less grain is used in producing yellow wine than white liquor, and yet the former has a higher nutritive value. If beer is called "liquid bread," then yellow wine can be called "liquid cake."

Omnipresence

Since the invention of wine, wine and liquor has penetrated every corner of society, adding color to people's life.

A Song Dynasty *Ying Qing* (misty blue) lotus-petal porcelain bowl for heating wine.

According to Chinese custom, one month after the birth of a child, the parents hold a feast to celebrate the completion of its first month of life. In a traditional wedding, the bride and groom drink "switched cup wine" from one another's red-lined glasses. People use wine to celebrate such happy events as promotions, victories, and birthdays. A common saying goes: "There is nothing but wine to assuage one's sorrow." Drinking wine relieves the summer heat, provides refreshment, and facilitates fun during one's spare time.

The Chinese have the custom of drinking wine during traditional holidays, such as Spring Festival Eve (30th day of the 12th lunar month), New Year's Day (January 1), Pure Brightness Day (early part of the third lunar month), Dragon Boat Festival (fifth day of the fifth lunar month), Mid-autumn Festival (15th day of the eighth lunar month), and the Double Ninth Festival (ninth day of the ninth lunar month).

In ethnic minority areas in southwestern China, wine is substituted for tea. When guests arrive, they are first offered three cups of wine. It's impolite if the guests decline the offer.

Once men of letters made friends with wine, it became a catalyst for the development of Chinese literature and art. It was said of the Tang Dynasty poet Li Bai: "A hundred poems flowed after cups of wine." The scholar Han Yu used to write while tipsy; the calligraphers Zhang Xu and Huai Su were called "Insane Zhang and Drunk Su." While inebriated, Zhang Xu would let himself go briskly writing on a white wall, whereas Huai Su would leave his handwriting on whatever wall or screen he wished.

Because of the literati's fondness for wine, wine became a permanent theme in literary and artistic creation. The first poetry anthology in Chinese history, *The Book of Songs* of the sixth century B.C., consists of 305 poems, of which more than 40 touch on wine.

Wine can be used not only as a beverage but also as a condiment called "cooking wine," which is used to eliminate fishy odors, and to enhance food color and flavor.

In traditional Chinese medicine, wine is used to reduce inflammation, relieve pain, relax the muscles, and stimulate blood circulation. As medicine, it can be used for external application, as well as for oral administration. Medicinal wine was introduced as early as the Zhou Dynasty. Some medicines should be taken with wine instead of water.

It is said that in a battle between the states of Chu and Jin during the Spring and Autumn Period (770-476 B.C.), when someone presented to the King of Chu casks of wine, the king poured it into the upper reaches of the river for his soldiers to drink, and, on the strength of the wine, the grateful soldiers pulled their full weight and defeated the Jin army.

From ancient times, wine, together with blood, has been used in China in swearing an oath of loyalty. For example, in 1935, while crossing the Daliang Mountain—home of the ethnic Yi people—during the Long March, the famous Red Army commander Liu Bocheng drank chicken-blood wine with a tribal chief to seal an alliance. An old saying goes, "A thousand cups of wine among congenial friends are too few, while one word in disagreeable company is more than enough." Because wine can enliven the atmosphere of a meeting and promote friendly relations, wine and wine-drinking have been considered by Chinese as a means of interpersonal and international communications.

(by Du Fuxiang)

Silk

With its long history, Chinese silk has been one of the oldest "envoys" of Chinese culture. As early as the third century B.C., when colorful Chinese silk made its appearance in West Asia and Europe, a king of the Western world was shocked to see before his eyes the fleecy cloud-like silk fabrics. It is said that a European emperor marveled at Chinese silk, exclaiming, "This is just like a dream!"

Suzhou is the generally recognized home of Chinese silk, or the silk capital of China. It is known to people who are interested in Chinese silk, that 90% of the genuine-silk trade in the world comes from China, and of the silk products exported from China, one third is from Suzhou. The large assortment of Suzhou silk, long known for its quality and beauty, finds a brisk market in more than 100 countries and regions around the world. It has been praised as a "mythical fairy."

Silk production in Suzhou has a history of more than 2,000 years. During the Western Zhou Dynasty (1046-771 B.C.), people in the Suzhou area began to grow mulberry trees, raise silkworms, reel silk and weave silk cloth. Later, Suzhou became the production and trade center in the Taihu Lake valley. In the latter half of the 20th century, silk industry attained a proportion never before known.

Tang Dynasty Silk: Beauty and Color

The Zijin Nunnery on Suzhou's East Hill is small and remote, but art connoisseurs have been attracted there to examine the 18 exquisite clay arhat statues, often carried away by the various facial expressions of the figures, to the neglect of their lifelike floating garments.

A silk expert once made some new discoveries here. He was amazed to find that the handkerchiefs in the arhats' hands, the garments draping over their bodies, and the canopy over the great merciful Bodhisattva Avalokitesvara, together with the red-flower adornments, were all of pure silk!

During the Tang Dynasty (618-907), Jiangnan Circuit (Suzhou being under its jurisdiction) presented more silk as tribute to the imperial court than other counties and prefectures, most of it being produced by Suzhou.

Bridges and Silk in Suzhou

As the "Venice of the East," Suzhou has a maze of bridges. Therefore, even stories of Suzhou's silk production is linked with bridges, as manifested in the following records of the silk textile workers in Suzhou of the 14th-19th centuries:

"In the east side of the city, almost all the people learned silk-weaving techniques. Weavers in Suzhou were paid by their regular employers on a daily basis…. Those without regular employers stood on a bridge early in the morning, waiting for their names to be called for work. There were cotton weavers and spinners as well as silk weavers. They gathered in groups of tens or hundreds and would disperse of their own accord if on a given day, no work was available. If there was not enough work, they could not feed and clothe themselves properly!"

There is a "Jiao Xie" (Call or Rest) Tablet beside Jiao Xie Bridge in Suzhou. Whether spinners could have work, and thus feed themselves, depended only on whether they were called by employers or if not, just rested. The rough tracks on the bridge might be workers' footprints while waiting for calls from employers.

The Romantic King of Wu: Brocade Sails

A dozen of Suzhou's street names are associated with silk, among which Jinfan (Brocade Sail) Road is the best-known. According to records, at the end of the Spring and Autumn Period, King Fu Chai (?-473 B.C.) of the State of Wu, once went on a spring cruise on a boat with a sail made of brocade. Some people are skeptical: can silk, so light and thin, be used as a sail on a boat? Scientists have proven that the stretching resistance of silk is equal to that of copper wire; thus parachute covers are made of silk.

According to records, officials of Wu all wore silk robes. There are also accounts of Wu people trading silk cloths and fabrics in the Central Plains. After the "Silk Road" was opened during the Han Dynasty, silk was transported to West Asia and Europe continuously from Suzhou.

Since the Song Dynasty (960-1279), silk centers had moved south. The Song court and those of the later dynasties set up special departments in charge of tribute silk production. In the beginning, Suzhou, Hangzhou, and Nanjing were equal in strength as silk producers, but why did Suzhou outshine the other two later? One senior silk craftsman explained, "There was definite division of labor among the three cities: dragon robes (worn only by the emperor) were produced in Nanjing; robes for ranking officials, empresses, and imperial concubines were made in Suzhou; and clothes of palace maids, eunuchs, and common officials were made in Hangzhou." Dragon robes used only by the emperors were needed less, so its place of production declined quickly; while production and marketing of Suzhou silk thrived because of its high quality and large quantity.

Today's Kimono and the Homophones

A Japanese scholar wrote in *The History of Textile Technique*, that "In the Qin Dynasty (221-206 B.C.), someone left Suzhou (called Wu at that time) for Japan to pass on the skill of weaving *hefu* (kimono)." *Hefu* (kimono) and *wufu* (or Wu robes) are homophonic in Suzhou dialect.

This is probably the historical origin of Wuxian County in Suzhou being the chief base for making kimono and obi for Japan.

Kesi weaving (a type of silk weaving done by the tapestry method) is another kind of artistic work in silk, and it is done completely by hand. First, vertical silk threads are set down. The outline of patterns and characters is woven on the background according to a draft. Colorful threads are woven into background horizontally. After the Song Dynasty, dragon robes were mostly made in the *kesi* style.

(by Feng Xuefeng)

Chinese Dress and Accessories in Various Periods

China has gained a reputation as "a country of fashion" with distinctive styles of dress associated with different periods of history,

The Beginnings

Ancient Chinese began to sew clothes 5,000 to 6,000 years ago when a primitive textile industry followed the appearance of primitive agriculture, and people began to lead a stable life. People spun thread from bast fibers on spinning wheels of stone or pottery, then wove the fabric to make clothes. From relics excavated from tombs, we know that decorative headwear and necklaces were made of various materials such as the skin and teeth of animals, fish bones, and shells. Clothes were designed not only for modesty and protection but also for a display of bravery, skill and achievements.

By the Shang Dynasty (c. early 17th century-11th century B.C.), Chinese had already acquired high technical skill in silk weaving. A new device for the loom was invented in this period to enable more complex patterns of weaving.

By the Zhou Dynasty (c. 11th century-256 B.C.), the dress of Chinese ancestors had tended to be bright and colorful. According to inscriptions on bronze ware as well as records in *The*

Primitive clothes.

Book of Songs and *Rites of Zhou*, the royal court set up a dress code with a special official in charge of implementing the code and attending to the king's wardrobe.

Colorful Dress in the Warring States Period

In the Spring and Autumn and Warring States periods (770-221 B.C.), the textile industry in both urban and rural areas produced more varieties of silk textiles along with more advanced techniques of weaving, dyeing and printing. The *gao* (a kind of white silk) produced in the State of Lu and the *xiu* (a raw silk fabric) of Chenliu in modern Henan Province were both famous in their time. And because the best textiles were found in the states of Chu and Qi, each came to be regarded as a "World of Fashion."

In an era characterized by great social changes, all schools of thought came into being, such as Confucianism, Taoism, and Legalism—and all these schools influenced how people dressed. Following the division of the Eastern Zhou Dynasty into many vassal states, different styles of dress characterized each state and people.

In the Spring and Autumn Period (770-476 B.C.), chariots were used in war. In the Warring States Period when wars extended from plains to mountain areas in north China, rulers of the states abandoned chariots for cavalry and infantry. "Hu Dress" (clothes worn by nomads or semi-nomads in northwest China and suitable for riding horses and shooting arrows) was closely associated with horsemanship and archery.

King Wuling of the State of Zhao (325-299 B.C.) decided to introduce "Hu Dress" to strengthen his military force, but his decision was opposed by some ministers who said it violated traditional rites. The king insisted that "laws and regulations should be as adaptable and suitable as clothes and weapons." The jacket, trousers and leather boots favored by the nomads then became popular in the Central Plains.

Gorgeous Dress and Accessories in the Qin and Han Dynasties

In the Qin and Han dynasties (221 B.C.-220 A.D.), people became more style-conscious and wanted more elaborate clothing. According to historical records, while Emperor Wendi of the Han Dynasty was on the throne (179-156 B.C.), in noble families even the servants wore expensive jewelry. In *The Roadside Mulberry,* a poem included in a Han Dynasty collection of folk songs and ballads, the hairstyle and dress of Luo Fu—a woman who was collecting mulberry leaves—was described:

> Her hair was done in a bun,
> Moon-like pearl earrings adorned her ears.
> She donned a light-yellow damask skirt,
> And wore a purple blouse to match.

The blouse reached to the waist and usually was worn with a hemless skirt made of four pieces of plain silk, narrow at the top and wide at the bottom, with two strings sewn to both ends of the silk top.

Men's garments in the Qin and Han dynasties could be divided into pleated and non-pleated. People of higher ranks wore robes, and officials usually wore robes without a lining. Robes had wide sleeves and open collars, both with bands. To facilitate their work, ordinary men wore tight

Han Dynasty clothes.

cotton jackets with narrow cuffs. A plain gauze robe unearthed from the No.1 Han Tomb at Mawangdui in Changsha, Hunan Province, was discovered to be "as thin and delicate as a cicada's wing and as light as smoke and fog," weighing less than 50 grams. Dating back to over 2,000 years ago, the robe is still strong in texture and brilliant in color. It demonstrates the excellent textile techniques of the Qin and Han dynasties.

Brilliant Fashions in the Tang Dynasty

During the rapid social and economic development of the Sui and Tang dynasties (581-907), feudal culture in the Central Plains witnessed its height of development. It was a period of wide cultural exchange and merging of social customs—including dress. For example, the attire of the flying Apsaras in the Dunhuang murals clearly originates from India. Popular jackets with a turndown collar were from northwestern peoples. The unification of the country with its thriving economy allowed innovations in textile technique and design. The variety of products, quality of weaving and sophistication of color reached new levels. Recorded materials included cotton cloth, thin silk, gauze, damask, silk gauze, brocade, and embroidered woven silk. Silk fabrics were discovered in recent years in such places as Turpan and Bachu of Xinjiang, and Dunhuang of Gansu Province—proof of the rich variety of textile design and excellent weaving and dyeing techniques of that time. Color analysis shows over 20 hues in the silk unearthed in Turpan.

With the developments in dyeing, textile, embroidery and silk weaving, the garment industry entered a flourishing period. The fine quality of fabrics, brilliance of colors, variety of styles,

Tang Dynasty clothes.

flamboyant designs, and skill of tailoring all reached a peak in the garment culture of feudal times.

Tang Dynasty garments were characterized by elegance, beauty and daring. Women's garments were mostly low-cut and of translucent silk or gauze. Women wore no undergarments, only wrapping a piece of gauze around them. Many Tang Dynasty women wore blouses and skirts. Makeup and hair ornaments were very important, with a rich variety of hairstyles and jewelry.

Tang Dynasty men wore robes with a round neck. Traditional ceremonial caps and garments were worn only on grand occasions such as sacrificial rituals. In everyday life men wore robes and head-coverings. Officials of different ranks wore different colors. Officials above the Third Rank wore purple, and those below the Third Rank and above the Fifth Rank wore red. The color of the Sixth Rank was green, and that of the Eighth and Ninth was black, which was later changed into bluish-green. This dress code changed in the reigns of later emperors.

Conservative, Simple Dress in the Song Dynasty

Generally speaking, the economy, politics, ideology and culture of the Song Dynasty produced a style of dress that was conservative, simple and quiet, with little variety in style, and duller colors compared with the Tang Dynasty. Yuan Cai wrote in his book *Social Standards*, "One should be dressed in clean, simple clothes. No clothes can be worn that do not conform to the generally accepted style." The emperors also reiterated that the people should "wear simple clothing," with "no lavishness or other noncompliance with dress code."

Song Dynasty garments were divided into official garments, men's wear and women's wear.

Women's garments were elegant, and tended to be loose with more variety in style. Women of that time loved the effect of "garments flowing in the autumn wind." Skirts were mostly made of thin silk or gauze. Long, floating dresses were popular, especially pleated dresses, which went beautifully with short, tight blouses. Noblewomen wore loose dresses with long, wide sleeves on ceremonial occasions. For casual wear, they favored long, more close-fitting dresses.

Unlike women's garments in Sui and Tang that were usually of primary colors with circular flower patterns, women's garments in the Song Dynasty displayed such soft and elegant colors as pale purple, greenish white, and silvery gray. Designs included twigs with blossoms, or balanced patterns, that looked lively and natural.

Song Dynasty women also wore a kind of "narrow-sleeved blouse," that was tight and formfitting, similar to the modern

Ming Dynasty clothes.

qipao (a close-fitting dress with high neck and slit skirt), showing off a woman's curves. Pleated long skirts were popular, which, in northern areas, could reach the ground, covering the feet.

As for men—civilians, servants and laborers wore black head-coverings; warriors, court officers in the judiciary, scholars, etc. wore head-coverings of different styles. Their robes buttoned in the front on the right, with wide sleeves and an apron around it. According to a person's social status, the border of the apron was decorated with gold, silver, jade, stone, copper, or horn-shaped objects.

In the Song Dynasty, the emperor and officials wore garments of the same style, which was different from other dynasties. Rank was determined only through different patterns and emblems on these same-style garments.

Clothing Style in the Qing Dynasty

Combining some features of Han customs and some of Manchu customs, the dress code of the Qing Dynasty style was the most complicated in Chinese history.

Men's garments included robes, outer garments, coats, shirts and

71

The imperial robe of a Qing Dynasty emperor.

trousers. Robes and jackets were major ceremonial garments. Officials and scholars wore robes with two splits at the bottom, while members of the ruling house wore robes with four splits and common people wore robes with no split. The cuffs were usually turned up, then were turned down when paying respect to a superior. Officials and wives of senior officials wore robes with python designs over their outer garments. Men's outer garments were generally reddish black, while those for funerals were black.

In the Qing Dynasty, the empress, imperial concubines and wives of senior officials wore phoenix headdresses and embroidered capes with tassels and emblems in the center. Ordinary women were allowed to wear these only at their weddings or at their funerals. Their ceremonial attire consisted of a cape, a blouse and a skirt. The cape was worn as an outer coat, and there were strict color regulations. Underneath the cape was a full blouse that could be unlined, lined, padded or leather. An undergarment was worn beneath the blouse that could be red, pink or cerise. Skirts were in many styles, which changed over time. Red skirts were regarded as the most elegant, but widows were not allowed to wear red. Some skirts were decorated with many small ringing bells.

Women's garments in the early Qing Dynasty were of quiet colors, decorated with narrow bands on the collar and cuffs. At the end of the Qing Dynasty, the bands were wider and more numerous. Some garments had fronts and lower hems decorated with floral patterns formed with jewels of various colors, or open patterns cut by scissors.

Common Traits

Some consistency exists in the styles, patterns and colors of Chinese garments even as they have experienced infinite changes throughout the millennia.

Basically all Chinese clothing can be divided into either one-piece garments or two-piece garments.

Garments before the Shang and Zhou dynasties were generally two-piece as were the garments of northern and western tribes and women's blouses and skirts of later times. One-piece garments appeared between the Spring and Autumn and Warring States periods, which were the predecessors of robes. In the history of clothes, two-piece garments were mostly women's wear and lasted for a relatively long time. Men after the Sui and Tang dynasties mostly wore robes.

Decorative patterns included animal, plant and geometric patterns that evolved through abstract, standard and realistic stages.

Patterns before the Shang and Zhou dynasties were similar to primitive Chinese characters, being simple and abstract. After the Zhou Dynasty, decorative patterns turned orderly, balanced and symmetrical. This was especially striking in the Tang and Song dynasties. In the Ming and Qing dynasties, patterns became realistic. Clusters of flowers, flocks of butterflies were depicted as lifelike. This feature was even more striking in the late Qing Dynasty.

The theories of Yin-Yang and Five Elements* influenced the colors of garments. Yellow, regarded as the noblest, symbolized the center; blue symbolized the east; red, the south; white, the west; and black, the north. These five colors were "principal colors," and in some dynasties were exclusive to the garments of emperors and officials. Common people were allowed to wear only secondary colors.

Looking at the overall history of fashion design in China, we can see

---

* The Five Elements (metal, wood, water, fire and earth) was a theory used by ancient Chinese philosophers to explain the origin of the world, by physicians of traditional Chinese medicine to make pathological diagnoses, and by superstitious people in fortune-telling.

that clothes of the remote ages were in relatively simple, bright colors, similar to the colors of pottery of the same period. With economic and cultural development, tastes about colors changed, and complicated, harmonious colors replaced bright, simple colors. Contrasting colors like red and green, yellow and purple, and blue and orange were used together less; while similar colors such as red and yellow, yellow and green, and green and blue were used more. Hues gradually turned more discreet and subdued, but still with some contrast. Garments generally displayed harmonious colors as a whole, with some accents of contrasting colors, for an overall elegant and splendid effect.

Drastic Changes in the Modern Era

China's failure in the Opium War in 1840 opened China to the outside world, and Chinese clothing came to be influenced by Western culture.

Young scholars bravely wore Western-style suits, abandoning robes and mandarin jackets and cutting their braids. In 1911, Dr. Sun Yat-sen led a bourgeois democratic revolution, or the Revolution of 1911, and the republican government promulgated an "Order on Cutting Braids," abolishing millennia-long traditions and rules on designating status by one's attire.

Toward the end of the 1920s, the republican government issued "Regulations on Uniforms," providing for the uniforms of men and women civil servants. The Chinese tunic suit became popular, a design based on Japanese students' uniforms. With a straight turndown collar, a single row of five buttons and a tight waist, it combined the convenience of Western suits and the comfort of Chinese garments. As it was popularized and worn early by Dr. Sun Yat-sen, it was regarded as a symbol of the democratic revolution and also known as "Sun's Suit."

In that period, Western suits and Chinese tunic suits were popular in major cities, where people were more open-minded, especially among the elite and intellectuals. In rural areas, ordinary people still wore robes and mandarin jackets.

Before the 1920s, women's garments remained two-piece, with little difference from Qing Dynasty garments. Shortly after the Revolution of 1911, as more Chinese students studied in Japan, the influence of Japa-

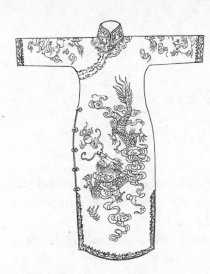

A modern *qipao*, or cheongsam.

nese women's wear on young Chinese women could be seen in a narrow, long blouse with a high collar and a long black skirt. Known as "modern garments," these clothes were accompanied by little jewelry.

In the 1920s, Chinese women started to be conscious of "the beauty of curvaceousness," and traditional straight, loose garments were replaced by close-fitting ones. Women of that period wore blouses narrow at the waistline, with small stand-up collars, sleeves reaching the elbows, and a curving hemline. The blouses were decorated on the collar, sleeves, front and hem. The skirts, which earlier had been pleated and reached the feet, were not pleated and shorter, though the hem still fell below the knees. The skirts were also decorated along the hem, sometimes with colorful, sparkling jewelry.

The major feature of modern Chinese women's wear was the *qipao*, which originated from the Manchu. After the 1920s, Han women started to wear *qipao*, changing and improving the original design until the *qipao* became common wear among Chinese women. The *qipao* became popular for two main reasons. Woman's attire previously had consisted of a blouse, trousers and a skirt. Now a *qipao* replaced all of them, and a *qipao* could be made at lower cost. Second, as a one-piece dress, the *qipao* set off a woman's figure, especially in high-heels.

(by Wu Yahua)

The Fan

Origin and History

In ancient times, Chinese ancestors found that waving a palm leaf in front of the body could create a cool breeze to clear the summer heat on hot days. That was the origin of the fan.

Before the fifth century B.C., most fans were made of feathers arranged on a bamboo frame. The function of those fans was not for cooling, but as the flags and embellishments for rulers and nobles. Thus fans could represent dignified manners and culture as well as keeping out the wind and sunshine. However, they had close relationship with the later fans and were the ancestors of the fans.

During the Warring States Period and the Qin and Han dynasties (c. fifth century B.C-third century A.D.), fans were no longer the monopoly of the nobles, but were used by people of all walks of life for cooling.

With the development of social productivity and silk-weaving technology, the quality of silk improved a lot. And fans made of bamboo strips, damask silk, or feathers, were all used by members of the ruling house and commoners alike. By the Western Han Dynasty (206 B.C-25 A.D.), silk fans had been used in the imperial palace. This kind of fans were round or oval-shaped with the bamboo or wood as the frame and covered with thin silks.

During the third century-sixth century, the folding fan and another cheap and functional fan, one made of Chinese palm, appeared. Also, another kind of fan was a silk fan topped with one or two strips of deer tail feathers, or bird's feathers.

In the Sui and Tang dynasties (581-907), with socio-economic and cultural development, fan production and fan culture also made great progress. The silk fan was the most popular style of that time. A silk fan with a wooden handle was excavated in 1973 in Xinjiang, dating back to the early Tang Dynasty. The face of the silk fan is circular, painted with two birds flying over two mountains, with a flower in their beaks. The handle of the fan is two and a half times the length of the fan's face, and its decoration is in the same style as those on the copper mirrors, fabrics and gold and silver articles of the same period. After the middle of the seventh century, most silk fans were round and were popular among women. Meanwhile, poems were written and pictures painted on the fans to express their feelings. Thus the functions of the fans were not only for cooling but also for art appreciation and adornment.

In the Song and Yuan dynasties (960-1368), silk fans were still the fashion, as shown in a special silk fan excavated in 1975 in Jiangsu Province. The carved lacquer handle of this fan is hollowed-out, with an axis in the middle that can rotate freely. Carved lacquer work was rare among archeological finds of that period, and this shows the high level attained in fan making. However, as silk fans could not be folded and carried along freely and were also expensive, they were gradually displaced by fans of paper and bamboo that could be folded and painted on.

The Song Dynasty saw the development and improvement of folding fans. The production of folding fans was on a large scale in Lin'an (modern Hangzhou), the capital of the Southern Song Dynasty. Folding fans then were used by common people and not objects men of letters would draw pictures or write poems on.

During the Ming and Qing dynasties and the Republic of China period (1368-1949), folding fans outshone other fans, becoming popular both among ruling houses and common people. Folding fans in these periods were integrated with calligraphy and painting, carving, embroidery, picture mounting and paper-cutting to become an art. They were produced all over the country and came in many styles, among which the black-paper fans made in Hangzhou and white-paper fans produced in Suzhou were the best-known of all.

During that period, silk fans had lost their favor with the general public, although in the late Qing period they gained some popularity, but only among noble ladies and men of titles. Meanwhile, feather fans also enjoyed some popularity, the best ones being produced in Huzhou of Zhejiang Province, Gaochun of Jiangsu Province, Yueyang of Hunan Province, and Honghu of Hubei Province.

In recent decades, fan manufacture has prospered. Many new products are sold all over the world. For instance, the Hangzhou Wangxingji Fan Factory manufactures over 10 million black paper fans and sandal-wood fans every year, which are much sought after not only at home but also in Europe, America and Southeast Asia. Besides, the carved ivory fans of Suzhou, the feather fans of Huzhou, the Gong fans of Sichuan and the Yueyang fans of Hunan are famed both at home and abroad for their exquisite workmanship and peculiar functions.

Although the traditional round fans, feather fans, folding fans and palm-leaf fans can not compare with electric fans in providing cool, they now have new functions. Manufacturers have developed the screen fans for decoration, the artistic fans and hanging fans for appreciation, the commercial fans for commodity promotion and the hat-fans that serve the two-fold purpose of shading the sunlight and providing breeze.

The Fan and Culture and Art

Chinese calligraphers and painters of all periods like to write poems or paint pictures on fans, thus fans became an integration of calligraphy, painting and handicraft.

In his *Art of the Fan,* the famous modern cartoonist Feng Zikai said, "The fan is one of the most advanced forms of calligraphy and painting in China." Since the Tang and Song dynasties, men of letters had opted to write poems or draw pictures on fans. The poems and paintings executed on fans by Tang Bohu, Shen Zhou, Wen Zhengming and Qiu Ying, the four great artists of the Ming Dynasty, and masters Ren Bonian and Zheng Banqiao of the Qing Dynasty, are all treasures handed down to posterity. The folding fan is broad at the top and narrow at the bottom and the paper is far from smooth. Thus to write Chinese characters and paint pictures on it is no easy matter. That's why artworks of this kind are all the more valued by connoisseurs.

The fan painting *Burning Incense Along the Bamboo-lined Ravine,* done by the painter Ma Yuan of the Song Dynasty, shows distant mountains and the near ravine, rock and bamboo, with an elderly man sitting on the rock before sticks of burning incense and a boy-servant scratching his head with one hand and holding a fan with the other behind the rock with lifelike expressions on his face.

A fan painting by Zheng Banqiao depicts a slender bamboo with several leaves in the autumn rain with free brushwork. He rounded off the painting with a poem describing the scene, written in strokes of primitive simplicity.

The fan also had close relationship with literature and art. Literati of all ages tended to express their feelings on the fans through poems. Lady Ban, a poetess in the Han Dynasty, wrote in her poem *Lament of the Autumn Fan,* "Fashioned into a fan, token of love/You are as round as brilliant moon above/In my lord's sleeves when in or out he goes/You wave and shake and a light wind blows." And as in the poem *An Autumn Night,* written by the famous poet Du Mu of the Tang Dynasty, "The painted screen is chilled in silver candlelight/She uses her silken fan to flap streaming fireflies/The steps seem steeped in water when cold grows the night/She lies to watch heartbroken stars shed tears in the skies."

The "plantain fan" in the classic Chinese novel *Journey to the West* is even used to fan off the fire on the massive Flaming Mountain, exaggerating the function of the fan out of proportion.

In the stage art, the different styles of the fans can set off the interest and character of the roles: With a folding fan hidden in the sleeve, the scholars look more elegant and cultured; fanning the palm-leaf fan, the hefty fellows from northwest China in the classical Chinese novel *Outlaws of the Marsh* look more bold and unconstrained; "a silk headdress on his head and a feather-fan in his hand," adds to the easy grace and elegant air of Zhuge Liang as a sagacious military strategist in another classical Chinese novel *Three Kingdoms;* and ancient Chinese paintings of young ladies in their boudoirs with round fans covering their faces set off their feminine modesty and beauty. Wielding a fan is a type of skill in traditional Chinese operas and is called "fan play." This is designed according to the personality, social status, profession and habits of the characters and has formed a whole set of regulations and orderly ways. The actors have concluded the following pithy formula: Scholars fan the head, warriors fan the abdomen, sedan-carriers fan the crotch, Buddhist monks or Taoist priests fan the neck, local tyrants fan the back, painters and calligraphers fan the sleeves, and the elderly fan the moustache.

A small fan can be used as a suppositional prop on the stage. With a fan in hand, an actor or actress can use it as if it were a knife or sword, a horsewhip or a writing brush. He/she can make the fan serve as letter paper when unfolding it; as a pillow when placing it under his/her head; as a carrying pole when putting it on his/her shoulder; and as a plate when holding it up with one hand.

The Fan World

There are thousands of types of fans manufactured in different places in China, the fan production kingdom. The mount of a fan is mainly made of some specific bamboo or wood, and the main materials to make the fan cover mainly of paper, silk or bird feather. Other materials include palm-leaf, wheat-straw and cattail leaf or stem.

Each fan-producing region has its own style, the most famous ones being those of Hangzhou, Sichuan, Suzhou, Yuezhou, Guangdong and Nanjing. And the Hangzhou fan is the best-known one.

In the fan museum in the Hangzhou Wangxingji Fan Factory, visitors can find a wide spectrum of fans. There are mini ivory fans (diameter 3.3 centimeters), super-sized screen fans (diameter 2.6 meters), black paper fans with a gold-painted picture, fans with paintings and handwritings by famous people, sandalwood fans, fan-dance fans, light fans, fine floss fans, peacock feather fans, and so on and so forth.

The Hangzhou Wangxingji Fan Shop (predecessor of the present Wangxingji Fan Factory), long known as the chief fan producer, was founded by the famous fan craftsman Wang Xingzhai in 1875. His fans used the "Three Stars" brand. Wang and his wife Chen Ying together developed three famous varieties of the black paper fan—golden-sprinkled, golden-painted and appliquéd—which, with their exquisite workmanship and fashionable designs, became Hangzhou's main tributes presented to the Qing imperial court. In 1927, the black paper fan manufactured by the Hangzhou Wangxingji Fan Factory was awarded a gold prize at the West Lake Exposition.

The "Three Stars" black paper fan is a traditional product known for its exquisite materials and consummate workmanship. To make a black paper fan involves a 86-step process. The mount of the fan is made of a special kind of bamboo and is soft and flexible and its cover is made of a special kind of paper pasted with a special kind of lacquer. And the fan will not get soaked in a rain nor become out of shape under a hot sun. The paper is durable and its color never fades. It can provide cool in hot summer and protection on rainy days. Hence the saying: "A 'Three Stars' fan in hand is half an umbrella indeed."

The first sandalwood fan was made by the Hangzhou Wangxingji Fan Shop in 1920. With lingering fragrance, it is a kind of handicraft with both use value and the value of appreciation. To make a sandalwood fan involves a process of scores of steps.

The tourists from home and abroad opt to buy Sichuan fans as a souvenir when they visit the area. Among local fans, the round silk fans and the bamboo fans are the most famous. The Gong fan, a bamboo thread fan produced by the Qing Dynasty craftsman Gong, is the best-known of Sichuan fans. The cover of a Gong fan is as thin as a cicada's wing. If you give a light flick to the mount of the fan, it will give out a musical "peng, peng" sound, a unique skill handed down from the Gong family. The cover of the fan is transparent and shiny and is decorated with pictographic patterns. This kind of fans has been presented by Chinese leaders as gifts to foreign heads of state.

The coastal areas of Fujian and Guangdong provinces and the island province of Hainan abound in Chinese fan palm (*Livistona chenensis*), whose leaves the local people use to make fans known as the palm-leaf fan. The palm-leaf fan produces a breeze much stronger than the feather fan, the silk fan or the folding fan. Besides being cheap, it can be used to drive away mosquitos, shelter from light rain and shade off sunshine, as well as to produce a breeze. The palm-leaf fan produced in Xinhui County, Guangdong Province, is the best-known of its kind. Xinhui County is called "home of palm-leaf fans," boasting a fan-production history of more than 1,600 years, dating back to the Jin Dynasty.

(by Sheng Jiuyuan, He Yaoying, and Mao Weidong)

Bamboo

Symbol of Nobility and Happiness

Bamboo originated from China and is the symbol of nobility and happiness in the minds of Chinese people. The Chinese character "*xiao* 笑" (smile) was designed according to the saying "Bamboo will bend in the winds like a man smiling." (The top part of the character "笑"means "bamboo," while the bottom part means "bending.")

China is a country with the longest history of using the bamboo. Legend has it that Goddess Nü Wa used bamboo to make musical instruments when she created the world by separating Heaven from Earth, that is to say, bamboo was born with the birth of mankind. And archeological finds have also proved that bows and arrows made of bamboo had been used in China 10,000-20,000 years ago. Several bamboo joints were discovered in the ruins of the 7,000-year-old Hemudu primitive society in Yuyao County, Zhejiang Province. The pottery artifacts from the ruins of the 6,000-year-old Banpo civilization in Banpo Village, Xi'an City, were found incised with the symbol "个," in the shape of a bamboo leaf. Such symbols have also been found in other cultural ruins. From this it can be seen that Chinese ancestors in the primitive society had begun to use bamboo and created

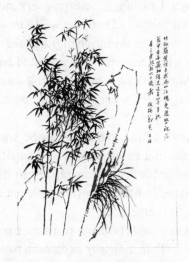

Orchids and Bamboo by Zheng Banqiao.

the pictographical character for it.

Bamboo has been omnipresent in the life of Chinese since ancient times. As early as in the Shang Dynasty (c. early 17th century B.C.-11th century B.C.), bamboo slips were used for writing and making bamboo articles; in the Han Dynasty (206 B.C.-220 A.D.), bamboo was used for building crude houses and in the Jin Dynasty (265-420), it was used for making paper. Su Dongpo (1037-1101), the great writer in the Song Dynasty, once described in an essay how the people in his hometown of Meishan in Sichuan Province used bamboo for food, for firewood, for building houses, and for making daily-use articles, clothes, writing paper, even shoes, and so on and so forth. He then concluded, "We can live without meat but not without bamboo; we will only become thin without meat, but we will become vulgar without bamboo."

The "Bamboo Civilization"

Bamboo had also played an important role in weapon making, irrigation works construction, mining, and textile machinery production in ancient China.

Well over two thousand years ago, Li Bing, a water conservancy expert, used bamboo in building the Dujiangyan Dam, the well-known irrigation works in Sichuan Province. With the invention of gunpowder, a firearm with gunpowder stuffed in a bamboo tube was invented and called "Tuhuo gun" in the Southern Song Dynasty; even the first water pipe in the world was made of bamboo, which was called "Jian" at that time.

In bamboo-yielding areas in south China, bamboo can be seen everywhere. A new-born baby was put in a bamboo cradle or carried around on the back in a bamboo basket; a bride was carried to the bridegroom's home in a bamboo sedan; and in funerals coffins were put in bamboo funeral sedans and carried to the cemeteries.

Being pliable, tough, straight, pressure- and corrosion-resistant, bamboo is ideal construction material. Many ethnic minority peoples in bamboo-growing areas in south China live in bamboo houses, such as those of the Dai people in Yunnan Province.

Meanwhile, bamboo also has significant potentials as food. Tender bamboo shoots are cooked in more than a hundred recipes in the southern and northern culinaries. Bamboo is also used in traditional Chinese medicine for clearing heat and resolving phlegm.

In his *Science and Civilization in China,* the British scholar Joseph Needham also told about the "bamboo civilization" in East Asia, how bamboo was put to many uses such as use as writing material in the Shang Dynasty, and how, in the Han Dynasty, characters were written on bamboo or wood slips and then held together with two ropes to make a "book."

Chinese characters were inscribed on tortoise shells or animal bones in the Shang Dynasty. From carving characters on bones or shells to writing them on bamboo or wood slips was certainly a big step forward in ancient civilization. Bamboo or wood slips came into fashion in the Spring and Autumn Period (770-476 B.C.)—mainly bamboo slips, wood slips being popular only in bamboo-deficient regions.

After bamboo took the place of bones and shells as writing material, ancient Chinese culture made huge progress.

With the development of society and the prosperity of culture, the heavy and expensive bamboo slips gradually became no longer able to meet the need of the people. Then paper was invented as the time required, in the second century B.C in the Western Han Dynasty. This was proved by the remnants of a paper map found dating back to the Western Han Dynasty at Fangmatan in Tianshui, Gansu Province. However, the paper produced in the Western Han Dynasty with its poor quality and small quantity could not yet replace bamboo slips altogether. In A.D. 105, Cai Lun, an official in the Eastern Han Dynasty, improved the paper-making method, to be followed by Zuo Bo at the end of the Eastern Han Dynasty. By then, the improved method was adopted nationwide. In the fourth century, after he had usurped the throne of the Eastern Jin Dynasty, Huan Xuan (369-404) ordered the use of the "yellow paper" (a kind of coarse, rough paper) in place of bamboo slips. Not until after another hundred years or so, approximately in the Southern Dynasties period (420-589), had paper completely replaced bamboo slips for writing on.

Although paper had taken the place of bamboo slips, still bamboo was indispensable in paper-making materials and tools. Even now when bamboo slips are no longer used, their cultural connotations and influence remain. In "Life of Li Mi" in *The Old History of the Tang Dynasty*, while listing the 10 major crimes of Emperor Yangdi of the Sui Dynasty, the author says, "even if we chop down all the bamboo in the southern mountains for writing material, it would still be difficult to give a complete list of his crimes." That's the origin of the Chinese idiom about someone's misdeeds or crimes being " 罄竹难书 " "far too numerous to record (on all the bamboo slips)."

Bamboo and Chinese Poetry and Painting

The green bamboo has attracted numerous painters and poets in all ages. Their poems and paintings, taking bamboo as the subject, have become an important part of the Chinese bamboo culture.

Poems on bamboo can be found galore even in *The Book of Songs*, the first Chinese anthology of poems, e.g. "Look at this land of Wei/The green bamboos, how graceful grown." "Gentle and smooth flows the stream/Quiet and tranquil stands the South Hill/It stands firm like clusters of bamboo/And luxuriant like pine groves green."

Poems and paintings about bamboo were even more popular in the Tang Dynasty. Xiao Yue was famous for his paintings of bamboo done in ink. The great poet Bai Juyi wrote a poem titled *Song to the Painted Bamboo,* "Looking up at it, I wonder whether it's a painting real/With all ears, I seem to hear the rustling of the bamboo leaves." Ink bamboo painting originated in the Tang Dynasty. Zhang Li once did one such painting on a wall in the Daci Temple in Chengdu, which added fame to the temple.

Poems about bamboo tend to represent the sound and waving of the bamboo, enhancing the charm of the poems. For instance, the lines by Wang Wei: "The bamboos rustle as girls return from washing/The lotus flowers stir as a fishing boat casts off." And Meng Haoran's lines: "The breeze brings fragrance from lotus fair/Dewdrops drip off bamboos with a splash clear," and Bai Juyi's lines: "The bamboo soughs and sighs before the house/While the stream under the house babbles."

More bamboo painters came to the fore in the Song Dynasty. Su Dongpo, the great poet, was a master of both bamboo painting and bamboo poetry; Su Guo, Su Dongpo's second son, was also adept at bamboo painting. The well-known sentence "You must have the image of the bamboo in the mind before you paint the bamboo" written by Su Dongpo in one of his essays was the origin of the Chinese idiom "成竹在胸" ("seeing the bamboo in one's mind's eye"), meaning "have a well-thought-out plan in mind."

Zhao Ji, Emperor Huizong of the Song Dynasty, was also good at painting bamboo. His famous painting "Listening to the Zither" has green pine trees and bamboo in the background.

Many poems and prose pieces were written about bamboo in the Song Dynasty. "The Newly Built Bamboo House in Huangzhou," by Wang Yucheng, is a famous piece of prose about a bamboo building and bamboo scenery. He wrote that one could find the beauty of a bamboo building "in a sharp rain in summer, sounding like a waterfall; in a fast snow in winter, sounding like the clicking of small pieces of jade. In a bamboo building, music from the zither sounds clearer and melodious. It's a good place for writing poems, for the rhymes are ringing and feverish. It's a good place for playing *weiqi* chess, for the pieces tinkle on the board. It's a good

A bamboo-encased porcelain tea set.

place for playing *touhu* (a game of throwing arrows into a wine pot), for the arrows clang when they hit the pot."

The "eight eccentrics of Yangzhou" in the Qing Dynasty all were excellent poets and calligraphers. They got the reputation of "eccentrics" because their painting styles were different from the so-called conventional style. Among them, Zheng Banqiao was an especially good bamboo painter. He also composed over 100 poems for his bamboo paintings. Here is the poem accompanying his painting "Bamboos and Rocks": "Holding tight to the green mountain/Taking root among the rough rocks/They remain tenacious in spite of incessant beating and striking/Or winds from north, south, east, and west."

Jin Nong, regarded as the first of the "eight eccentrics," started learning painting at 58. He started by painting bamboo and then Chinese plum flowers, horses, and Buddha. His bamboo paintings in ink are fresh, simple, and unadorned in style. Most of the "eight eccentrics" were good bamboo painters and made outstanding achievements in the history of bamboo painting.

Gao Qipei, a Qing Dynasty artist, painted bamboo with his fingers. His works show a unique style and highly developed skill. His painting "Bamboo and a Bird," masterpiece of ancient Chinese finger painting, shows a slender bamboo and a bird perching on one of its branches, making it full of the tang of life.

Bamboo is an important subject of traditional Chinese poetry and painting. With a straight, hollow stem, bamboo is looked upon as a symbol of the unbending spirit of the Chinese nation, and together with the pine and plum as "the three friends of winter," which do not wither in winter.

Interesting Species

China has four million hectares of bamboo forests, accounting for one fourth of the world's total bamboo forest area. China produces five to seven million tons of bamboo annually, ranking first in the world. China has the largest number of bamboo species of any country in the world. Among the over 1,000 bamboo species of the 62 genera in the world, nearly 300 species from 26 genera have been found in China.

There are many interesting bamboo species in China. The square bamboo, for example, has a square stem with rounded angles. It can be found in Jiangsu, Zhejiang, Guangdong, Sichuan, Fujian, and Taiwan provinces, and the Guangxi Zhuang Autonomous Region. The square bamboo has been popular since ancient times, but its production is limited. Square bamboos can also be produced artificially by encasing 20-centimeter-tall bamboo shoots inside a square wooden column. The production of artificial square bamboos has developed greatly in Taiwan. Many utensils and handicrafts made of square bamboo, such as tea trays and pen containers, are popular and sell well because of their unique style.

The soft-textured giant reed is the only material for producing musical instrument, and is therefore a very valuable bamboo species.

The mottled bamboo is a well-known species. It is so called because, as legend has it, in the remote past when Emperor Shun died, his two wives, Ehuang and Nüying were so sad that their tears fell on bamboo plants and left permanent marks. Thus, the mottled bamboo became a subject for praise through history. As a Tang Dynasty poem on the mottled bamboo goes: "Emperor Shun traveled south and never returned/The sorrow of his two wives filled the sky from the water to the clouds/How many pearl-like tears did they shed/The bamboo still bears their stains." Today mottled bamboo is produced artificially by applying sulfuric acid to bamboo stems.

The "giant dragon" bamboo, produced in Xishuangbanna, Yunnan Province, is known as the king of bamboo. Giant dragon bamboo plants can grow to upwards of 20 meters in height, with a diameter of over a meter.

The dwarf among bamboos is *sasa tortunei*, which grows to a maximum height of only about 20 centimeters. It can be grown in pots as an ornament.

Dwarf bamboo species can be grown in pots after being artificially stunted. The ideal species for stunting is the fernleaf hedge bamboo. The secret is: when the bamboo grows to 12 centimeters in height, pinch off the tender tip at the top of the shoot to stop the bamboo's growth.

The black bamboo, the rarest bamboo species, is entirely black with a shining stem and branches. Its opposite is the chalk bamboo, which is white like jade.

Bamboo Handicrafts

The bamboo has thousands of uses, and handicrafts are possibly the most lovely.

Gong Yuzhang of Zigong, Sichuan Province, is known as "Fans" Gong because he makes beautiful bamboo fans. He weaves fans with bamboo threads as thin as hair, so that they are as thin in texture as silk. He also weaves various patterns in his fans by making use of the shiny and rough sides of the bamboo threads. The art of "Fans" Gong is a gem of the Chinese bamboo craft.

The production of bamboo fans has a history of over two millennia in China.

Among the works of Chinese bamboo weaving art, the bamboo mosquito nets of Sichuan are regarded as the acme of perfection. They are transparent and bear patterns of flowers and birds.

The woven bamboo animals and human figures of Yu Zhanggen, a bamboo weaving artist, are well known abroad. One of his works, a bamboo vulture, attracted much attention at the World Exposition in Tennessee, in the US. An American company presented it to the then President of the United States. "Ma Gu Presenting a Birthday Gift," another work of Yu's, is even more exquisite. The work comes from a fairy tale: The fairy Ma Gu presented wine to the Heavenly Queen Mother for her birthday. It shows Ma Gu carrying a round tray with wine and peaches on it, flying lightly and gracefully out of the clouds. Her features are clear and vivid. It is an excellent example of the craft of bamboo weaving.

In Taiping, Anhui Province, there are several hundred kinds of bamboo weaving products, of both traditional and new designs, including flower baskets, trays, insect cases, and figures of animals and birds. These products are exported to Europe, America and other parts of Asia and are popular in the international market.

Many places in China produce woven bamboo products. Fujian Province is an important one. Ningde, Fujian, is well known for pillows made of thin bamboo strips, which sell well overseas for their softness and elasticity. In Quanzhou, Fujian Province, the main woven bamboo products are flower baskets, vases, and ancient-style pots. Some are lined with pottery and can be used to contain water or grow flowers. The bamboo surfaces of such products have undergone antiseptic treatment. Yongchun County produces items combining bamboo weaving and lacquer, which are much sought after in the international market.

In Tunxi, Anhui Province, bamboo weaving started in the Tang Dynasty. Today, the production has changed much in variety and technique. The products include containers, baskets, screens and mats, all of delicate craftsmanship.

Bamboo carving is a handicraft with a long history in China. Bamboo root carving, the art of carving bamboo roots into sculptures based on their natural shapes, is appealing for its combination of nature and human workmanship. Hunan, Sichuan and Zhejiang styles are the three main bamboo-carving styles in China. Bamboo carving in Shaoyang, Hunan Province, has a history of just over 100 years, but its products now come to nearly 200 varieties. The bamboo ware items from Shaoyang have a variety of colors and bear carvings of landscapes, flowers, birds, animals, human figures and stories. They are unique in design, lovely in motif, and harmonious in color; they show a combination of traditional and new carving techniques.

The production of bamboo mats goes way back in China. The Chinese character for mat in oracle bone script from several thousand years ago is "▦," a pictographic character consisting of a rectangle and a woven pattern. It shows that the form of mats has not changed much over the millennia.

Summer sleeping mats are both for everyday use and ornamental use, mostly woven with *Phyllostachys congesta*, a bamboo that is tender, fine, dry and straight, with few joints. Mats woven with such bamboo are soft, smooth, comfortable, and cool. There are many famous types of bamboo mats in China. Some mats, woven with thin bamboo strips of *Phyllostachys congesta*, have pictures of vivid human figures, landscapes, animals, calligraphy, buildings, or stories.

Bamboo is an ideal material for making various musical instruments. Ancient Chinese people started to make musical instruments with bamboo long ago. Most Chinese wind instruments are made of bamboo, the best-known being *sheng* (a reedpipe wind instrument), *xiao* (a vertical bamboo flute), and *di* (an eight-holed bamboo flute). Many Chinese ethnic minorities also produce their own bamboo musical instruments. The panpipe of the Li in Hainan Province, made of two thin bamboo tubes, produces a rustic sound.

Bamboo engraving is the art of carving Chinese characters and images on bamboo objects. The smooth, fine texture of bamboo makes it ideal for engraving. The oldest engraved bamboo object found so far is a colorfully painted bamboo ladle handle bearing a dragon pattern, unearthed from a Han Dynasty tomb at Mawangdui in Changsha, Hunan Province.

Engraved bamboo calligraphy is usually an imitation of famous calligraphers' works. Jin Xiya, a contemporary bamboo-engraving artist, was famous for his perfect imitation of various calligraphers. His engraved paintings are also unparalleled. In his old age, Jin wished to record his life experience in bamboo engraving, and entrusted the task to his nephew Wang Shixiang. Together they published *The Art of Bamboo Engraving* in the 1980s.

(by He Yangming)

Chopsticks

Two sisters of the same height,
Together they go in and out of the kitchen.
Sour, bitter, or spicy, a thousand flavors,
They are always the first to taste.

The answer to this riddle is chopsticks. A traditional Chinese eating utensil, chopsticks have undergone a long history of development and become a symbol of traditional Chinese food and drink culture and representative of Eastern civilization. They are also used in other countries, especially Japan, Korea and Southeast Asia.

History of Chopsticks

Chopsticks are utensils for picking up food. When did they appear? Who invented them?

According to legend, Yu invented chopsticks 4,000 years ago when he was taming the Yellow River. He had to eat meals in the field. When he was in a hurry, he could not wait for food to cool and had to pick up the hot food with twigs. Hence chopsticks were invented.

According to historical records, chopsticks have a history of at least 3,000 years. Few bamboo and wood chopsticks have been found among unearthed cultural relics, because they rot much faster than bone, jade and metal chopsticks. The earliest chopsticks extant were unearthed from a tomb of the State of Chu during the Spring and Autumn and Warring States periods over 2,000 years ago.

The Great Variety of Members of the "Family of Chopsticks"

At first, chopsticks were made of bamboo or wood. Later, there appeared ceramic, copper, iron, gold, and silver chopsticks. Today, the development of science has added many new members to the "family of chopsticks."

Copper chopsticks were the earliest metal chopsticks. They fell out of use in the Tang Dynasty, when they were banned, because copper oxidizes easily and becomes poisonous. Silver replaced copper and was popular among feudal rulers, high-ranking officials, and rich merchants, who believed the silver would discolor if the food was poisoned. However, modern scientific research has shown that silver chopsticks are not reliable poison indicators. Only poisons containing sulfur turn the surface of silver chopsticks into black silver sulfide, and substances containing sulfur are not necessarily poisonous. On the other hand, toxins containing no sulfur, such as fugutoxin and nitrate, do not discolor silver chopsticks.

Gold chopsticks were used exclusively by the royal family. They were so expensive that common people and ordinary officials could not afford them.

Today, there are a great variety of chopsticks. The most famous chopsticks include geranium chopsticks from Zhejiang, *nanmu* chopsticks from Sichuan, lacquered chopsticks from Fujian, appliquéd chopsticks from Hubei, and white wood chopsticks from Jiangsu. Beijing artists have produced high-grade chopsticks of hardwood, red copper, and jade, using techniques of cloisonné, carving and inlaying. Some bamboo or wood chopsticks are printed with various patterns or famous lines of poems, or engraved with the 12 zodiac animals.

Cultural Characteristics

Chopsticks have deeply influenced many aspects of traditional Chinese culture throughout the millennia of history. It has its own subculture, the culture of chopsticks.

Chopsticks etiquette is an important part of Chinese manners. In ancient times, Chinese society observed a strict hierarchy among the emperor, officials, and commoners. Any breach of the system would be punished by jail and even the death penalty. Gold chopsticks, symbolizing imperial power and honor, could only be used by the royal family.

Ordinary banquets also had complicated etiquette. There were 10 taboos in using chopsticks: first, hesitating while holding chopsticks in the air; second, picking up food from the bottom of the dish first; third, piercing food with chopsticks; fourth, tearing fish or meat in the mouth with chopsticks; fifth, picking food from soup; sixth, picking teeth with chopsticks; seventh, sucking on chopsticks; eighth, standing chopsticks vertically in a bowl of food; ninth, knocking a bowl or the table with chopsticks; and tenth, pointing at someone with chopsticks. In most families, young children were taught these rules early on.

In China, chopsticks have been regarded as auspicious since ancient times. In some areas, chopsticks are used in certain customs.

Scattering chopsticks was a wedding custom in ancient times among the Han people of Hunan Province. When the bridal sedan set out, the bride's family scattered chopsticks in the courtyard, praying to their ancestors for the bride's happy married life. The Chinese word for chopsticks sounds the same as "soon," so scattering chopsticks implies, "have a son soon."

Shouldering chopsticks was a wedding custom of the Achang people, popular in the Dehong Autonomous Prefecture of Dai and Jingpo, Yunnan Province, among other places. The "chopsticks" are actually a pair of newly cut thin bamboo stems about two meters long. The bridegroom stays at the bride's home overnight and eats breakfast with the "chopsticks" the next morning before taking the bride away. The bridegroom carries the chopsticks with shaky hands or puts them on his shoulder. The breakfast consists of special foods such as deep-fried peanuts, rice noodles, and bean curd, which are hard to pick up with chopsticks. The bridegroom is often soaked with sweat before finishing breakfast.

Shifting chopsticks was a wedding custom of the She people in Zhejiang Province. Before the bride gets into the sedan, firecrackers are lit and a square table is set in the central hall of the bride's home, with displays of sacrifices to ancestors and a large bowl of rice. On both sides of the bowl are pairs of chopsticks equalling the number of the family members. An elderly man of the same clan recites a speech, to the effect that so and so is getting married and will live in such and such a place, wishing for the ancestors to bless her, and so on. After the speech, the bride's brother carries her into the central hall and puts her on a stool. Then the ceremony starts: the bride takes up the bamboo chopsticks from the table, crosses her arms behind her and passes the chopsticks to her brother standing behind her, who replaces the chopsticks onto the table from under the bride's arms. At the same time, all the people present sing the "Song of Shifting Chopsticks," wishing her happiness with her husband's family.

Hanging chopsticks was an old custom of the Han people in southern Hebei Province during the construction of houses. On the day when the roof beam is to be laid, chopsticks tied together with a red string are hung from the post over the front door, with five red strips of cloth hanging from them. Firecrackers are lit at the same time for good luck. The chopsticks hang for 49 days before being removed. In this custom, the chopsticks represent bones of evil spirits; the red string, their tendons; and red cloth strips, their five internal organs. Today, the custom is rarely observed, and only firecrackers are lit when the beam is laid.

Chopsticks are also used in Chinese dances. The Mongolian chopstick dance is mostly a solo dance for men in Inner Mongolia. The dancer hits himself with the chopsticks on the shoulders, hands, waist, legs, feet, and sometimes the ground while dancing. His shoulders and waist move harmoniously while he spins or kneels. The dance features masculine movements and strong rhythms. Recently, variations on the dance make it a group dance performed by men and women together.

Bamboo and wooden chopsticks are easy to carve. Carved bamboo chopsticks from Jiang'an, Sichuan Province, are famous in China and overseas, and have won many international prizes. Carved chopsticks, which began in the 17th century, are made of *mao* bamboo (*Phyllostachys edulis*), which is thick and has long sections, in a complicated process. Chopsticks finely carved with lions on their tops are well known throughout China. A chopstick may bear a single lion, a pair of lions, a lion standing on a treasure, or a mother lion and her cub. Wooden chopsticks are also good materials for carving. Chopsticks engraved with green pines, turtles, and cranes, which represent longevity, are good birthday gifts for elderly people. Bamboo and wooden chopsticks can also be burned with patterns. Wu Tian, a Qing Dynasty chopstick artist, burned patterns of animals and landscapes onto chopsticks with a heated, sharp carbon pen. Chopsticks could increase in value 100-fold after he burned them.

Dining with chopsticks is convenient, safe, hygienic, and good for physical and mental health. Modern science has found that while one is using chopsticks, over 30 joints and over 50 muscles are used, which is a favorable stimulation to the brain. Dr. Tsung Dao Lee, a famous Chinese-American physicist, favors chopsticks. He said, "Such a simple pair of sticks show a marvelous utilization of the lever principle. Chopsticks are extensions of the fingers, able to do anything fingers do. They can be used in heat and freezing cold. They are wonderful." Today, more and more people around the world use chopsticks. Westerners in China for the first time are often proud of themselves for being able to use chopsticks like the Chinese.

(by Wang Xinxi)

Traditional Chinese Musical Instruments

An important member of Chinese culture, traditional musical instruments have developed vigorously, like a towering tree with deep roots and luxuriant leaves, abundant flowers and excellent fruit.

When humans in China first began to use tools thousands of years ago, they also fashioned crude musical instruments from stone, wood, and other materials. With social and technological progress, over 500 varieties of musical instruments have been created with steady improvement and winnowing. A complete family of traditional Chinese musical instruments has taken shape, whose shapes and structures, performing skills and sound integration are characterized by complementarity and deep artistic expressivity. Here, we introduce some common traditional musical instruments: *sheng*, gong, *huqin* and *pipa*.

Wind Instrument—*Sheng*

Sheng is a musical instrument made of reedpipes of various shapes, including circular and square ones, in a frame. To play the *sheng*, one covers the finger holes and vibrates the reeds by blowing. It is an important wind instrument of the traditional Chinese instruments ensemble with unique artistic charm.

As one of the oldest musical instruments in China, the *sheng* was the first instrument in the records of history after the appearance of the written language. During the Spring and Autumn and Warring States periods, King Xuan of the State of Qi would ask 300 people at a time to play the *yu* (a kind of *sheng*) for him. The recluse Nan Guo volunteered to join the royal orchestra. The king accepted his offer happily, and gave a banquet for the hundreds of players. King Min, who succeeded the throne after King Xuan died, preferred to listen to a single *yu* player. The recluse fled on hearing the news. This is the popular idiomatic phrase of "pretending to play the *yu* in order to make up the number of an orchestra," reflecting the historically grand occasions for playing the *sheng* (*yu*) during the Spring and Autumn and Warring States periods. The performance of the *sheng* was greatly improved during the heyday of the Tang Dynasty. The *sheng* even spread to Europe over the Silk Road in the 18th century.

Playing the *sheng*, a reedpipe wind instrument.

With the scientific and technological development, the structure of *sheng* has improved. For example, copper has replaced bamboo reed to solve the problem of intonation. The initial 13 pipes have gradually been increased to 17 and then 24, expanding its range and enriching its harmonies.

To meet the needs of the development of the traditional musical instruments, the *sheng* has occupied an increasingly important position in the orchestra. A great number of players have innovated to strengthen the *sheng's* artistic expressivity. *Sheng* players in the Central Traditional Instruments Orchestra increased the original 32 reeds to 36, further broadening the range; added an audio amplifier to make the high pitches clear, melodious and bright, and the low ones simple and vigorous; and divided the half-tone sequence into 12 tones in three groups to achieve flexible transposition and well-developed choruses. The transformed *sheng* can play not only traditional Chinese musical compositions, but also Western masterpieces of music.

Gong—A Percussion Instrument

The gong is one of the percussion instruments among China's traditional musical instruments. According to historical records, the *sha* gong during the Southern and Northern Dynasties period (420-589) is the ancestor of today's Chinese gongs. The copper gong unearthed in Luobo Gulf of Guixian County in the Guangxi Zhuang Autonomous Region is the earliest gong so far known. According to textual research, it has a history of over 2,000 years.

The gong is a circular copper percussion instrument of various sizes, to be struck with a stick. The smallest one can be held in one's palm, while a large one must be carried by two persons. As an indispensable component of the various opera accompaniment orchestras and instrumental ensembles, it produces an instantly recognizable artistic effect.

There are many varieties of gongs. Their names vary according to the shapes, sizes, scopes of use, high or low pitches and tone colors. The gong used in Peking opera, which is called the "Beijing gong," is small, making clear, melodious, sonorous and bright sounds; the "lion gong," which is only 10 cm in diameter, may be placed on the left palm and struck with thick bamboo sticks by the right hand; the "black gong," whose name originated from its appearance—the edges and center of it are painted black, is used by folk honor guards to clear the way, so it is also called the "gong to clear the way"; and the name of the "tiger-sound gong" originated from its sound as of the roar of a tiger. Other types of gongs can be found in different areas.

Foreigners usually call the large gongs that are 50-120 cm in diameter "Chinese gongs." With their simple and vigorous tone color, which is dignified, deep, sad, and powerful, it can be integrated into music of various types. Due to its strong artistic expressivity, it is especially favored by composers. In ancient times, "large gongs were beaten to clear the way" for officials on tours of inspection; when engaging in a battle, two hostile armies would "beat drums to bolster the soldiers' morale, and clang gongs to withdraw troops"; gongs were also used in folk activities, such as grand festivals, weddings, and funerals, to add a magnificent atmosphere to the scene.

The art of making gongs is very complicated. In spite of constant scientific and technological progress, large gongs are still cast by hand by experienced workers through a manual striking process. As the saying goes, "A gong is produced through a thousand strikes, but the music is determined by one strike"; in other words, only the stroke when completed can determine the quality of the gong.

Gongs are widely used in Chinese opera. For example, the sound of the murmuring river, as imitated by gongs in the Peking opera *Autumn River*, is quite lifelike, as if the actors are leisurely rowing a boat on the blue water.

Modern composers especially favor the special sound effects of large gongs. The deep and strong effect produced by their vibrations is often used to express meditation, grief or sinister omens, making a great impact.

With the development of cultural exchange, Chinese gongs and their artistic effects have spread to countries around the world. Large gongs used by European orchestras after the 16th century originated in China. Nowadays, some famous symphony orchestras of Western Europe, the United States, Russia and other countries and regions boast Chinese gongs.

Huqin—A Stringed Instrument

The earliest Chinese stringed instrument appeared in the Tang Dynasty; to make a sound one rubbed the strings with bamboo slips. It was not until the Song Dynasty (960–1279), comparatively late in history, was there a record of an instrument with horsetail strings.

Shen Kuo, a famous scientist of the time, noted a "horsetail *huqin*" in China's northern border area. In ancient times, the people in the Central Plains called all ethnic minorities living in western and northern China the *hu*, or "the northern tribes"; therefore, their musical instruments were collectively called *huqin*. The horsetail *huqin* refers to a stringed instrument with a horsetail bow.

People began using stringed instruments to play solos during the Song Dynasty, reaching a fairly high

An *erhu* (fiddle) solo.

level of performance skill. An old story took place at that time: An artist named Xu Yan was asked to play a solo with *jiqin* (a stringed instrument) at a palace feast. A string suddenly broke as he just started to play. With his rich performance experience, Xu Yan went on playing calmly with only one string, completing the music skilfully.

The Mongolian ethnic group unified the entire Central Plains area during the Yuan Dynasty (1279-1368). They brought the traditional culture of the northern ethnic minorities to the Central Plains, gradually integrating the two cultures. The stringed musical instruments were constantly improving and developing during the process of exchange, and a new *huqin* with a curling neck, dragon-shaped head, two strings and a horsetail bow slowly took shape. Stringed instruments like the *huqin* became popular during the Ming Dynasty (1368-1644). They gradually became the most important musical instruments in the accompaniment of various operas, songs and dances.

Due to their various shapes and materials, *huqin* are divided into many varieties. Stringed instruments are made with locally available resources and reflect the interests and characteristics of the various ethnic groups. Although each stringed instrument has its own name, *huqin* has always been used to generally refer to the various stringed instruments.

The reform of Liu Tianhua, who revolutionized traditional music in the early 20th century, led to a major leap in China's stringed instruments. Using the various popular *huqin* as a basis, he invented a new instrument, the *erhu*. He composed repertoire for it, reflecting contemporary intellectual thoughts and interests, and compiled 45 etudes for it, freeing it from the level of a folk art and bringing it to the musical institutions of higher learning. He thus built the foundation for the artistic specialization of Chinese stringed instruments. Since then, other stringed instruments have been popularized greatly, and entered the institutes of higher learning. Composers have produced a large repertoire for it, such as Liu Tianhua's ten compositions (which include *Chanting While Sick* and *A Bright Trip*), *The Moon Over a Fountain* and *Listening to the Sound of Pines* by the folk musician Ah Bing (Hua Yanjun), and hundreds of other works by various composers. Many have also arranged well-known pieces for the *erhu*, further increasing its popularity.

Pipa—A Plucked String Instrument

Pipa is the oldest and most famous plucked instrument in China.

There were two kinds of *pipa* during the Qin and Han dynasties. One had a straight handle and round sound box, and animal skin covered the two sides. It could be plucked and strummed with the fingers, and it was called the "Qin *pipa*" by later generations. The other also had a straight handle, round loudspeaker box, but was vertically plucked with a plectrum. It was called the "Han *pipa*" and "Ruanxian" by later generations. Approximately in the mid-fourth century, a *pipa* with a crooked neck spread to China from India. Chinese musicians of various ethnic groups reformed its performances by integrating the performing skills of the Han *pipa* and making innovations, and the present *pipa* gradually took shape.

"Still covering half her face when playing the *pipa*," goes the famous verse of Bai Juyi, a great Tang Dynasty poet, vividly depicting the appearance of a *pipa* player. Bai Juyi wrote many verses about the *pipa*, among which the *Song of a Lute Player* was most striking. In the 10th year (A.D. 815) of the Yuanhe period during the mid-Tang Dynasty, Bai Juyi

was appointed assistant magistrate of Jiujiang Prefecture. He saw off a visitor on the bank of the Xunyang River while feeling lonely and helpless one day, when "suddenly hearing the sound of the *pipa* on the water, the host forgot to return home and the guest stopped to listen." The versatile poet was at once deeply attracted, and he wrote the famous verse: "The girl came out at last after being called a great many times, still covering half of her face when playing the *pipa*." According to records, the *pipa*-playing girl from the capital city used a "Han *pipa*" and played with a plectrum.

Playing the *pipa* (lute).

103

Among all the *pipa* repertoire, *Ambush on All Sides* has had the widest popularity among most people and places. As one of the five principal representative works of *pipa* music, it depicts the historical story of the ambush masterminded by Liu Bang to defeat Xiang Yu when the states of Chu and Han confronted each other. By using the special fingerings of the *pipa*, the music vividly depicts a fierce battle scene. It begins with Liu Bang discussing military affairs in his tent, then calling the roll of officers and assigning them tasks, deploying the troops in battle formation, and setting up the ambush, and all the large and small engagements during the campaign. Liu Dehai, a modern *pipa* master, has played the music in dozens of countries and regions, causing a great sensation wherever he went. Dumbfounded, an audience in Paris could hardly believe that a single musical instrument could depict such a magnificent, large-scale battle scene.

The *pipa* plucked string instrument has undergone thousands of years of transformation and development. With the many followers throughout the nation, the *pipa* is highly favored by many.

Chinese stringed instruments can be divided into those played horizontally and those played vertically. The *guqin* is played horizontally, while the *pipa* is played vertically. Besides the *guqin*, *se* (psaltery), and *zheng* are the similarly shaped horizontal instruments. The Chinese proverb, "The *qin* lute and *se* psaltery are in harmony," refers to the close bond between friends. The *se* is a 25-stringed plucked instrument with a support under the strings to muster the pitches. The tone color is particularly beautiful and touching.

The *zheng* circulated in the State of Qin (the present Shaanxi area) during the Warring States Period, therefore, it was also called the

A solo on the *zheng*
(a kind of Chinese zither).

qinzheng. It was a popular 12- or 13-stringed instrument tuned to a five-tone scale during the Tang Dynasty.

The *zheng* was a popular instrument with a simple structure, and it was played by people of all social strata. Like other instruments, the *zheng* had different styles and schools due to undeveloped communications, local language differences, and differing geographical environments.

Besides the *pipa*, the vertically played instruments also include the *ruan*. The frequently used large and medium-sized *ruan* play important parts in traditional orchestras.

Playing the *zhongruan*, a medium-sized tenor variety of *ruanxian*.

The *sanxian* is a common three-stringed plucked instrument of the Han, Mongolian, and other minority ethnic groups. The small *sanxian* is mostly used for accompaniment in Kunqu opera; while the large one as accompaniment for the northern *quyi* (Chinese folk art forms, including ballad singing, story-telling, comic dialogues, and clapper talks), *dagu* (versified story sung to the accompaniment of a small drum and other instruments), and *danxian* (story-telling by singing to musical accompaniment). Due to its unique tone color, it was later made a part of traditional orchestras, achieving an excellent effect.

Due to its shape, which resembles a salix leaf (*ye*), the *liuqin* is also called *liuyeqin*. It is a major instrument in the music of the local operas in southern Shandong and northern Jiangsu, playing a high-pitch part in traditional orchestras.

All these instruments have created magnificent and colorful musical culture from China's remote historical ages to the present.

(by Hui Ping, Lu Wei, Xiao Xinghua, and Liu Xiaoqi)

The "Four Treasures of the Study"

The "four treasures of the study"—writing brush, ink stick, ink slab and paper—are writing tools with a long cultural tradition and unique artistic style created by the ancestors of the Chinese nation. They have played an important role in recording Chinese history, popularizing various cultures, and promoting the development of Chinese calligraphic and painting art over thousands of years.

With socio-economic and cultural development, the varieties of writing brushes, ink sticks, ink slabs and paper have all increased. The skills of craftsmen and production technologies have likewise constantly been improving since the Jin (265-420) and Tang (618-907) dynasties. They have formed their own artistic tradition and discipline in their designs, which have become works of art in themselves.

The term *wenfang* (secretarial section of a government office, or a study) originated during the Southern and Northern Dynasties (420-589), when it referred to the unit overseeing the state's cultural activities. Since the Tang and Song (960-1279) dynasties, it has been used to refer specifically to the scholar's reading and studying room.

The "four treasures" are characterized by great variety and rich content. Many famous articles and masters of eminent reputations can be found in history, such as the Hu brush from Huzhou County in Zhejiang Province (the old Huzhou Prefecture); Duan ink slab from Gaoyao County in Guangdong Province (the old Zhaoqing Prefecture, named Duanzhou during the Sui and Tang dynasties, the present Gaoyao County being under the jurisdiction of Zhaoqing City); Xuan paper from Jingxian County in Anhui Province (under the jurisdiction of the former Xuancheng Prefecture); and Hui ink from Shexian County in Anhui Province (the old Huizhou Prefecture).

Writing Brush

The writing brush has a long history in China. In the beginning, people wrote with bamboo sticks on bamboo slips. Around the time of the Warring States Period 2,200 years ago, the ancient Chinese began to tie rabbit hair to bamboo sticks to make the first writing brushes. The brushes of the early period were crude and simple, while later ones made of a mixture of deer hair and wool are characterized by the correct stiffness and good workmanship.

The manufacturing of writing brushes has been constantly improved and perfected with the progress of the Chinese culture. Besides rabbit hair and wool, people also used fox, wolf, and chicken hair, as well as mouse whiskers, to make brushes of varying stiffness.

Writing brushes from the Han Dynasty (206 B.C.-220 A.D.) were unearthed early. For example, a brush of the late Western Han or the early Eastern Han Dynasty was found in an ancient house in Yanze (present Ejin Banner, Inner Mongolia Autonomous Region) of northwest China in 1931. It was made of a shaft of four long wooden sticks tied together by hemp thread at the top and bottom, with black hair and a white tip. The shaft was made of wood, because bamboo was scarce in northwest and north China at that time. Among the writing materials unearthed in a tomb of the Western Han Dynasty on Phoenix Mountain in Jiangling, Hubei Province, the writing brushes with bamboo shaft were very similar to the ones of the Qin Dynasty.

Most of the unearthed writing brushes were ordinary writing

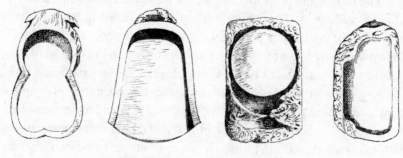

Ink slabs made of Songhua stone.

instruments; those used by members of the nobility were often exquisitely decorated, either with gold-inlaid shafts or mounted gemstones on the caps. It is said that a single writing brush was worth up to 100 *liang* (5,000 grams) of gold.

The technology of producing writing brushes was carried on during the Wei and Jin period (220-420). A calligrapher named Wei Zhongjiang was universally acknowledged as an expert in this field. In the Jin Dynasty, Xuancheng was known for the writing brush made of brownish rabbit hair from Zhong Mountain, characterized by firm hair and skilled craftsmanship. These brushes were greatly admired by scholars. According to Bai Juyi, the great Tang Dynasty poet, "The writing brush made of brownish rabbit hair is as keen as an awl and as sharp as a knife. It is made of the hair of old rabbits on mountains in regions south of the Yangtze River, which live on bamboo and spring water. The workers in Xuancheng collect the hair to make the brush, choosing one in 10 million. Light as it is, it plays an important role—the workers contribute it as annual tribute…." Therefore, the "writing brush made of brownish rabbit hair" was a treasure of such high quality that it was sent to the imperial court as tribute at that time.

The writing brushes from the Huzhou area of Zhejiang Province were well known during the Ming and Qing dynasties (1368-1911), which were made of goat, rabbit, chicken, or wolf hair, and whose nibs were pliable and tough with moderate elasticity. They were superior to *xuan* brushes. The writing brushes had a multitude of names, and their shafts were mostly made of expensive materials. Therefore, they were not only used for stationery, but also for their artistic value.

The development of the writing brush was of great importance to Chinese calligraphy. The quality and type of the writing brush had a great impact on the calligraphy of the ancient scholars; depending on the brush, the writing could be serious and pointed, dignified and imposing, bold and vigorous, or graceful and smooth. Calligraphers were very particular about choosing their writing brushes. Legend has it that once there was an ancient calligrapher who made his own brushes. He would make a hundred, then choose the best few, break them up and combine the best parts of each into a single writing brush. He wrote whatever he wished with the brush that could last five or six years.

New writing brushes are not necessarily good for writing. According to experienced calligraphers, "Big characters written with small writing brushes are too thin, while small characters written with big writing brushes are too thick." People could only write bold and vigorous characters with the writing brushes without pointed tips. Therefore it is said, "An inch of gold will not buy a bald writing brush."

Although nowadays people can write easily with pens and pencils, which are easy to carry, none of them can replace writing brushes, which still hold the lingering charm of traditional Chinese culture.

Ink Stick

The quality of the ink stick is greatly important for calligraphers. Good-quality ink not only enables calligraphers to evenly moisten their brushes, but also to make their writing dark, dignified, solid, and serious. Naturally, calligraphers are very particular about ink stick selection. Chinese painters also use the ink in painting and dilute it to create a contrast between dark and light shades.

The appearance of the ink stick provided a necessary condition for the invention of printing in later ages. Therefore, both the ink stick and the writing brush have made great contributions to the development of Chinese culture.

Artists often engrave paintings and Chinese characters on ink sticks. A stick of high-quality ink brings together the skills of painting, calligraphy, sculpture, and ink making.

The invention of the ink stick is an oft-told folk tale in China. Xing Yi was born during the reign of King Xuan of the Western Zhou Dynasty (?-782 B.C.). One day, while washing his hands in a brook, he found a piece of charcoal in the water. Picking it up, his hands were stained black. In a sudden flash of inspiration, he brought the charcoal home, crushed it into fine powder, blended it with rice and other bonding materials, then shaped it into flat, round cakes. Thus the first ink stick was invented.

At first, the ancients made ink sticks with "black earth," or graphite. Later, various other kinds of materials were incorporated into ink sticks, such as pine shoots, lacquer, and lampblack. Their shapes varied from a ball shape to a rectangular bar, which is still the standard today.

Depending on the ingredients used, the different types of ink take different characters. Ink made from pine shoots is heavy and dark; lampblack, dark, bright, and solid; and lacquer, dark, simple, and vigorous. Su Dongpo, a famous scholar of the Song Dynasty, regarded "ink with pure gloss that does not drift, and as clear as the eyes of children" as the top-grade product.

Great advances were made in the quality and modeling of ink sticks during the Qing Dynasty. The ink used in the imperial court, such as the Sanxitang and Momiaoxuan varieties, were valuable works of art. Commoners usually used Longmen, Lanyan, Wannianzhi, and Jinbuhuan ink. Besides ink sticks used for writing, there were also "ink sticks for thoughtful appreciation" and "housekeeping ink sticks," the latter of which was frequently given as a gift to relatives and friends. The "housekeeping ink sticks" were packaged in a complete, elaborately decorated set, designed with great originality. Such ink sticks were engraved with famous sayings of the ancients, floral patterns, or landscape scenes. Such designs were simple but elegant. Musk and perfume were added as well. Such top-quality ink sticks are now highly prized by collectors, who regard them as art treasures.

Although pre-mixed ink is both popular and convenient to use when writing calligraphy, it is much inferior to freshly prepared ink from ink sticks. Many painters and calligraphers still use ink sticks for appropriately thick, smooth ink which produces best results. The traditional treasure of the study cannot be replaced.

Paper

Before paper was invented, ancient Chinese used heavy bamboo slips, expensive silk, or cattail leaves for writing. The appearance of paper was a major turning-point in human history, for it eased writing itself, was easy to transport, and was inexpensive. Thus, the invention of paper greatly promoted human scientific and cultural exchange.

Archeologists have discovered many relics, showing that people began to use hemp and other vegetable fibers to make paper as far back as the Western Han Dynasty (206 B.C.-24 A.D.). The earliest paper was too rough to completely replace bamboo and silk; it was not until Cai Lun's innovations that paper was widely used.

Cai Lun was a eunuch who was responsible for making household items used by the imperial court during the reign of Emperor Hedi (r. 88-106 A.D.) of the Eastern Han Dynasty. According to historical records, "He made paper with bark, hemp heads, rags, and fishnets." Another version states, "Cai Lun pounded old fishnets to make paper, and named it net-paper." The method of making paper by pounding raw materials into pulp was called "beating." Through this process, Cai Lun drew out the pure fiber to make paper, which was characterized by few contaminants and a bright white color. The so-called "Cailun paper" was well adapted for writing.

During the Eastern and Western Jin dynasties and the Southern and Northern Dynasties period, China's papermaking industry developed rapidly. Papermakers used a wider range of raw materials and improved production technology. The paper industry spread throughout the entire country during the Sui and Tang dynasties (581-907). Paper varied in quality due to the different raw materials and manufacturing processes used. The "hemp paper" of Yangzhou in Jiangsu Province and "Xuan paper" of Xuanzhou in Anhui Province, started to enjoy high reputations.

Xuan paper is a top-grade paper for brush writing. Its name comes from the city of its production, Xuanzhou. It is made with the pulp of tree bark and rice grass, treated with lime, bleached by sunlight, and beaten. Its pure white color, delicate feel, and durability—it is moth- and water-resistant—makes it well adapted to use and storage. Most of ancient and modern calligraphic works and paintings were, and are, done on Xuan paper.

Besides Xuan paper, long the standard, Maobian (literally "hair-edge") paper also enjoys a good reputation. It became very popular in the Ming Dynasty (1368-1644). The name does not mean that the edges were covered with hair, but is a reference to Mao Jin, a book collector of the late Ming Dynasty. To cut costs while printing large quantities of ancient books, he did not use Xuan paper, but a new type, whose edges were printed with the character "mao." People then called it Maobian paper. The Xuan paper that he used is properly called "Shengxuan," characterized by strong absorbency, which was suitable for calligraphy and freehand brushwork in traditional Chinese painting. When Shengxuan paper is soaked in alum water, it becomes Shouxuan paper, particularly good for meticulous painting. It was an indispensable annual tribute of local officials to the imperial court.

During the Qing Dynasty (1644-1911), new raw materials were used in manufacturing Xuan paper. From using 100% tree bark, new varieties of paper were made from 100, 70, or 50% bark. The difference was made up with rice straw, which both increased the output and quality of Xuan paper.

The Xuan paper of the Qing Dynasty consisted of more than 20 varieties. During the reign period of Jiaqing (r. 1796-1820), paper handicrafts made in China were sold to various regions in Western Europe and became very popular there.

Ink Slab

An old saying goes, "The ink slab is as important to the scholar as the field is to the farmer." The ancients believed that the ink slab was of great importance among the "four treasures of the study." Intellectuals regarded a precious ink slab as a treasure handed down from antiquity.

So far, no conclusion has been made on the earliest origin of the ink slab. A stone ink slab was found several years ago in a tomb of the initial Yangshao cultural period (5,000-3,000 B.C.) in Jiangzhai Village, Lintong County, Shaanxi Province. The ink slab's stone cover concealed a concave hollow for ink. A total of five pieces of black pigment (manganese monoxide) and gray pottery cups beside the ink slab constituted a complete set of colorful earthenware. It indicated that the abrasive utensils were used as calligraphic and painting tools as far back as the later period of the primitive society 5,000 years ago. These were the ancestors of today's ink slabs.

What is the best material for making ink slabs? During the Han Dynasty, ink slabs were made from jade or pottery; during the Tang Dynasty, pottery ink slabs became popular, and the famous clear-mud ink slabs, made of pottery baked with a special mud, first appeared. It was also during the Tang that Duan, Xi, and Zhaohe stones were used.

There were no regular-height tables and chairs before the Tang Dynasty. Instead, people had to read and write on low tables while kneeling on mats. Ink slabs were placed under the tables. To adjust to the situation, they were mostly circular or dustpan-shaped, with feet, and no distinction was made between the area for grinding ink and the ink well itself so that it could hold as much ink as possible. Propped up by the feet on only one side, the surface of an ink slab was slanted to easier brush-dipping.

High tables and chairs appeared in the late Tang Dynasty. Ink slabs were moved from under the small tables to the surface of the high tables. Platform ink slabs thus increased gradually.

Valuable, high-quality ink slabs were not easy to obtain, for they were usually hidden among huge rocks, and people had to discard layers of wasted stones to obtain the treasures. Ink stones were also difficult to distinguish from other stones. Thus finding ink slabs was no easy task.

Engraved ink slabs became common during the Song Dynasty. Artisans became expert at selecting stones for such work and incorporating natural lines in the stone into the pictures. Most of the famous ink slabs of the Song Dynasty were engraved with figures, flowers, and grass, or the inscriptions of scholars. Some semi-relief figure sculptures were striking in their perspective. Innovation in the Song Dynasty period brought higher artistic levels to ink slabs.

Among the stone ink slabs of the Yuan Dynasty is a peculiar one unearthed in Beijing, called the "stone warmer ink slab." It has two parallel ink wells with hollow chambers underneath, in which a fire could be lit to heat the stone ink slab, preventing the ink from freezing in the winter. In the Qing Dynasty, metal and porcelain ink slabs appeared, in whose foundations fires could be lit to warm the ink.

During the Ming Dynasty, most of the ink slabs were made of Duan stones, which were highly praised by scholars and calligraphers. They were exquisitely and meticulously engraved. Although some Duan stones were even smaller than a human palm, craftsmen hated to part with them and engraved the dainty Duan ink slabs by following their shapes.

During the Qing Dynasty, because Emperor Qianlong loved the "four treasures of the study," special workshops were established in the imperial palace to recruit highly skilled craftsmen to make ink slabs. Besides the capital city, production centers were gradually established in Anhui, Guangdong, Jiangsu, Zhejiang and some other provinces, each with its own style and employing a number of highly skilled craftsmen.

During the Ming and Qing dynasties, the production of ink slabs became even more artistic. They were meticulously carved with varied and colorful pictures, and engravings and inscriptions on ink slabs became especially popular. The most elaborate ink slabs greatly exceeded the practical applicability of stationery, and become simply art objects.

(by Su Honghong, Fang Wen, and Xu Chen)

Chinese Ceramics

As you know, the English word "China" refers both to our country and to porcelain. Porcelain is one of China's best-known great inventions, to the point that both porcelain and the country have the same name.

China was one of the earliest civilizations to produce ceramics, and pottery was widely used in many fields of life in remote ages. Pottery was used to make food and wine vessels and other containers; dippers; musical instruments (such as the pottery *xun* and pipe whistle); tools (such as the pottery spindle, grid drop and sickle); and burial objects—both coffins and vessels interred with the dead. With the development and progress of the material life of human society, ceramics are used to make lamps, tea sets, drinking vessels, spittoons, pillows, toys, ink slabs, water basins, penholders, screens, and ornamental containers for plants and animals, now taken for granted in the material and spiritual lives of human society.

The infinite shape possibilities of ceramics and the ability to decorate ceramic surface with pictures made ceramics a natural choice for artistic creation. People made ceramics not only for their practical needs, but also to beautify their lives. Among the ancient relics of the Neolithic Age (approximately 10,000-4,000 years ago) are a great

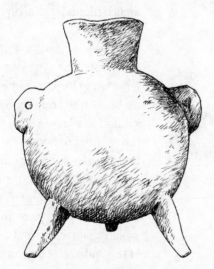
A primitive three-legged pottery ewer.

number of the painted pottery and pottery figures of the ancient Chinese people. Ceramics reflected people's customs and tastes through their shapes, decoration, and glaze colors. Therefore, ceramics were not only commodities of people's material lives, but also a material souvenir of their intangible lives.

Historical Origins of Chinese Ceramics

Many pieces of pottery of the primitive society were excavated from China's Yellow and Yangtze river valleys, notably the Yangshao, Majiayao, Dawenkou and Longshan cultures of the Yellow River valley and the Hemudu, Daxi, Qujialing and Liangzhu cultures of the Yangtze River valley over 6,000 years ago. Painted pottery gradually fell out of favor, while black, white, gray, and red pottery continued to develop and change in the succeeding period of time.

The Shang Dynasty (16th century-11th century B.C.) witnessed the beginnings of workshops producing commercial pottery, including gray, white, and stamped pottery. During the Zhou Dynasty (11th century-third century B.C.), the pottery industry further grew, and ceramic building materials, such as arched tile and railing bricks, appeared.

Gray pottery was the most common type of pottery during the Qin and Han dynasties (third century B.C.-second century A.D.), but red and black pottery were also popular. Ceramic building materials became increasingly important to the pottery industry, among which stone reliefs and eave tiles were the most distinctive.

A painted pottery duck from the Warring States Period.

The Qin Dynasty Terracotta Warriors and the Tang Tricolor

Great advances were made in pottery figures during the Qin and Han dynasties. For example, the true-to-life Qin Dynasty terracotta warriors excavated in Shaanxi Province have become a world-famous artistic monument. Although not as magnificent as the Qin Dynasty terracotta warriors, the pottery figurines of the Han Dynasty were exquisitely made. During the Han Dynasty, artisans mastered the art of glazing pottery.

During the Tang Dynasty, a new low-temperature glazed ceramic called the Tang tricolor was developed. Existing examples of the Tang tricolor have mostly been excavated from tombs, especially in Henan Province, where the technique originated. Frequent discoveries in this field have been made in various areas of Henan since the first dig took place in Luoyang in the early 20th century. Luoyang continues to rank first in both quality and quantity of Tang pieces. Many of the tricolor pieces unearthed in Henan are figurines of northern Chinese tribes leading camels. The camels sometimes are shown carrying silk or serving as backups without loads. Some hold their heads high as they look into the distance; others stretch their necks and neigh while walking. Scenes of friendly contacts between the Chinese of the Tang Dynasty and people from all parts of the world are another motif of the Tang art. Besides tricolor camels, tricolor horses and figurines are also well known. The Tang tricolor declined rapidly during the middle and late Tang, but revived later during the Northern Song.

The tricolor glazed pottery produced during the Song Dynasty (960-1279) is called the Song tricolor. Those of the Liao Dynasty (916-1125) were

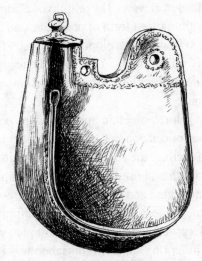

A coxcomb glazed reddish-brown pot with two holes, from the Liao Dynasty.

117

A polychrome teapot from the reign of the Ming Dynasty Emperor Wanli.

often decorated with engraved designs.

Fahua pottery, a variety with embossed designs, appeared during the late Yuan Dynasty (during the mid-14th century). Such relief pottery has a striking effect to the eye, and became popular after the Ming Dynasty. During the Ming and Qing dynasties, Yijun pottery was produced in the Yixing area of Jiangsu Province. Most Yijun products were an attractive sky blue. Boccaro pottery also became world-famous.

Porcelain

The main categories of Chinese porcelain are celadon, black, white, and colorful ware. The primitive celadon of the Shang and Zhou dynasties was the earliest form of porcelain, and the art of celadon matured over the 1,700 years of development between the Shang and Eastern Han (in the early third century A.D.). Han Dynasty porcelain is as fine in quality as modern porcelain. Black porcelain appeared during the Eastern Han Dynasty.

White porcelain appeared approximately 400 years after the emergence of celadon in China. This rather late emergence can be attributed to two factors: the raw materials of white porcelain were more difficult to obtain than those for celadon and its production process was both more complicated and difficult. Nevertheless, we can never know for certain. In the context of historical and cultural tradition, the Chinese have long had a psychological taboo against pure white. White is the traditional color for mourning apparel. This taboo was obviously unfavorable to the early development of white porcelain. Some have speculated that gray-glazed porcelain, discovered in an Eastern Han Dynasty grave in Changsha, Hunan

Province, is actually a forerunner of white porcelain. However, it is indisputable that there was no further development of white porcelain for another 300 years. It was not until the Northern Qi Dynasty (550-577) during the late Northern Dynasties (386-581) period about 400 years later that true early white porcelain emerged as the next major advance in the porcelain industry. Its art matured during the Sui and Tang dynasties.

The Tang Dynasty was a time of unprecedented development—political, economic, and cultural—for the Chinese feudal society, and the porcelain industry was no exception. During this period, China began to export porcelain to foreign markets. Different porcelain kilns producing various styles appeared, such as the Yue Kiln of Yuezhou (present-day Shaoxing, Zhejiang Province) and the Xing Kiln of Xingzhou (present-day Neiqiu, Hebei Province). The practice of naming kilns after their locations lasted into the Song, Yuan, and succeeding dynasties.

In the spirit of their forefathers, the people of the Tang Dynasty improved the quality of porcelain remarkably, producing not only celadon ware, but also white, black, and colored porcelains. Celadon and white porcelains were the two large sectors of Tang porcelain production. The Yue Kiln was known for its celadon; the Xing Kiln for its white porcelain. Besides these two, the kilns of Wuzhou, Dingzhou, Yuezhou, Tongguan, and Shouzhou were also well known. The elegant and harmonious spotted glazed porcelain was also produced during the Tang Dynasty. Such utensils were dark-glazed and covered with lighter flakes of color. During the Five Dynasties period (907-960), the production scale of

An exquisitely wrought blue and white porcelain plate.

celadon at the Yue Kiln expanded, and the varieties of porcelain produced also increased. The imperial "olive green Yue ware" was produced there.

Five Famous Large Kilns

The Song Dynasty (960-1279) was an important stage in the development of Chinese ceramics. Song porcelain was mature both in the shapes and decorations as well as the techniques of manufacture. The varieties of porcelain and the system of kilns far exceeded those of the Tang Dynasty. Besides celadon, white and black porcelain, there were also shadowy blue porcelain, white porcelain with a pattern of black flowers, red glazed and flambe porcelains. The major porcelain kilns included Yue, Wu, Tongguan, Yaozhou, Cizhou (present Cixian County, Hebei Province), Jingdezhen (in Jiangxi Province), and five famous large kilns—Ru Kiln (present Linru, Henan Province), the Northern and Southern Guan Kilns (present Kaifeng, Henan Province and present Hangzhou, Zhejiang Province, respectively), Ding Kiln (present Quyang, Hebei Province), Ge Kiln (present Longquan, Zhejiang Province), and Jun Kiln (present Yuxian County, Henan Province).

The Liao and Jin dynasties were regimes established by ethnic minorities, the Qidan and Nüzhen peoples. Therefore, despite the closeness in time between their ceramics and Song porcelain, Liao and Jin ceramics retained local ethnic features.

Jingdezhen Blue and White Porcelain

With improvements in manufacturing techniques, the porcelains of the Yuan Dynasty (1279-1368) were thick and heavy, and many new varieties appeared. The white porcelain of the Yuan Dynasty, characterized by close texture, solid structure, and highly regular shape, was a great achievement. The blue and white porcelain, actually a white porcelain with blue floral patterns, produced at Jingdezhen in Jiangxi Province was a landmark in the history of Chinese ceramics. Blue and white porcelain first appeared during the Tang and Song dynasties, but attained maturity in the late Yuan Dynasty. The designs of blue and white porcelain reflected the spirit of the times, and

A traditional blue and white porcelain vase.

a variety of shapes or patterns were engraved or painted on the objects. A red underglaze porcelain was also produced in Jingdezhen, which was a white glazed porcelain with a red floral pattern. Its effect was achieved by painting red flowers on the base ceramic before coating with glaze.

The development of Chinese ceramics reached its peak during the Ming and Qing dynasties. Jingdezhen became the center of the national porcelain manufacturing industry during the Ming Dynasty, and Cizhou in Hebei Province, Dehua in Fujian Province, and Longquan in Zhejiang Province also boasted unique products. In addition to white-glazed porcelain with a black flower pattern, white porcelain, and celadon, blue and white porcelain had become the mainstream. During this period, porcelain of "contending colors" appeared, produced by outlining with blue on the roughcast, applying white glaze, entering the kiln, filling in colors, and firing twice. The blue-and-white outline and the filled-in colors enhanced and complemented each other's beauty, hence the name. During the reign periods of Jiajing and Wanli of the Ming Dynasty, new porcelains were produced by directly painting with colors on the fired products instead of outlining in blue. Characterized by rich and beautiful colors, they were called "hard-colored" or "five-colored" porcelain. Famous porcelains included the "*tianbaiyou*" (sweet white glazed porcelain) of the reign periods of Yongle and Xuande, an ingeniously-shaped white porcelain with a thin roughcast, the yellow glazed porcelain of the Hongzhi reign period, and the green glazed porcelain of the Zhengde reign period.

During the Qing Dynasty, five-colored porcelain attained consummation. The products of the Kangxi reign period were characterized by a splendid tone and great skill in figure painting. The large porcelain plate *General Yue's Army Fighting the Jin Troops*, on display in the

Pea-green porcelain wine vessels.

Palace Museum, is a consummate work of art. Mixed glaze appeared during the Kangxi reign period, which was painted with colors blended with lead powder, characterized with natural colors, clear gradations and a strong three-dimensional effect. To distinguish it from hard colors, it was called "soft color." The contents of painting mainly included flowers, birds, insects and butterflies. Cloisonne enamel, another new product of the Kangxi reign period, was characterized by its fine texture, high cost, and low output. Called "Guyuexuan glaze," it was mainly a toy in the imperial palaces. Great importance was attached to ceramics in the Qing Dynasty, promoting the development of the porcelain manufacturing industry.

China suffered from the invasions of Western powers for over 100 years since the mid-19th century, and as a result, the people lived in destitution. The porcelain industry likewise declined. Since the establishment of New China, the old ceramics trade has gradually revived, many traditional crafts have recovered, and new techniques have constantly surfaced. The porcelain industry has developed vigorously throughout the country.

图书在版编目(CIP)数据

中国传统文化 ABC / 文珍珠主编.
—北京：外文出版社，2005
ISBN 7-119-03904-0

I. 中... II. 文... III.传统文化—简介—中国—英文
IV. G12

中国版本图书馆 CIP 数据核字(2004)第 140095 号

责任编辑：朱英煜
封面设计：蔡 蒙
插图绘制：李士伋
中插摄影：吕 岩

外文出版社网址：
http://www.flp.com.cn
外文出版社电子信箱：
info@flp.com.cn
sales@flp.com.cn

中国传统文化 ABC

文珍珠 主编

*

©外文出版社
外文出版社出版
(中国北京百万庄大街24号)
邮政编码 100037
北京藏文政印刷厂印刷
中国国际图书贸易总公司发行
(中国北京车公庄西路35号)
北京邮政信箱第399号 邮政编码 100044
2005年(大32开)第1版
2005年第1版第1次印刷
(英)
ISBN 7-119-03904-0/G·12(外)
01800(平)
7-E-3693P

图书在版编目（CIP）数据

中国传统文化 ABC / 文郭湘主编.
—北京：外文出版社，2005
ISBN 7-119-03904-0

I. 中… II. 文… III. 传统文化—简介—中国—英文
IV. G12

中国版本图书馆 CIP 数据核字（2004）第 140098 号

责任编辑　李淑清
封面设计　蔡　荣
图形绘制　李士伋
印刷监制　张国祥

中国传统文化 ABC
文郭湘　主编

*

© 外文出版社
外文出版社出版
（中国北京百万庄大街 24 号）
邮政编码：100037
北京冠华印刷厂　印刷
中国国际图书贸易总公司发行
（中国北京车公庄西路 35 号）
北京邮政信箱第 399 号　邮政编码　100044
2005 年（大 32 开）第 1 版
2005 年第 1 版第 1 次印刷
（英）
ISBN 7-119-03904-0 / G·83（外）
01800（平）
7-E-3869P